Alphabet on Parade

Preschool
Ages 3–5

March into beginning literacy with fun activities
for skills such as the following:

- Letter Identification
- Identifying Beginning Sounds
- Identifying Beginning Consonants and Vowels
- Making Letter-Sound Connections

Written by: Jean Warren

Managing Editor: Cindy Daoust

Editorial Team: Becky S. Andrews, Kimberley Bruck, Karen P. Shelton, Diane Badden, Sharon Murphy, Kimberly Brugger-Murphy, Leanne Stratton, Susan Walker, Allison E. Ward, Karen A. Brudnak, Sarah Hamblet, Hope Rodgers, Dorothy C. McKinney

Production Team: Lisa K. Pitts, Pam Crane, Clevell Harris, Rebecca Saunders, Jennifer Tipton Bennett, Chris Curry, Theresa Lewis Goode, Ivy L. Koonce, Clint Moore, Greg D. Rieves, Barry Slate, Donna K. Teal, Tazmen Carlisle, Amy Kirtley-Hill, Kristy Parton, Debbie Shoffner, Cathy Edwards Simrell, Lynette Dickerson, Mark Rainey

How to Use This Book

Young children are always eager to sing, talk, and play their way to literacy when we provide them with developmentally appropriate opportunities to learn. That's what this book is all about! It includes an array of letter and sound ideas that three-, four-, and five-year-olds will love. Because all children develop at different rates, select ideas to use with your youngsters that best match your observations about their current developmental levels and understandings. If you see an idea that's just a little too challenging for some of your children today, return to it in a few weeks. By then it may be just right for them.

Table of Contents

www.themailbox.com

©2004 The Mailbox®
All rights reserved.
ISBN10 #1-56234-623-7 • ISBN13 #978-156234-623-2

Manufactured in the United States
10 9 8 7 6 5 4 3

The Letter A

The Ants Go Marching

The ants go marching over *A*s in this fine-motor activity, which will help develop letter awareness and letter-sound correspondence. Duplicate onto construction paper the letter *A* pattern on page 9 to make a class supply. Cut out a pattern for each child. Provide an ink pad that has washable black ink and a small ant rubber stamp. Write the word *ant* on the board and point out the letter-sound connection. Next, encourage a child to stamp ants onto his letter *A* cutout as he softly repeats the word *ant* or makes the short *A* sound. Display the ant-covered *A*s on a red-and-white checkered background. The ants go marching over *A*s. Hurrah! Hurrah!

Apple Pal Puppets

These friendly apple stick puppets are a welcome addition to any *A* unit! Duplicate onto red construction paper the apple pattern on page 9 to make a class supply. Cut out the apple shapes and give one to each child. Provide each child with two wiggle eye stickers. Next, invite her to use markers and crayons to draw facial features on her apple cutout. Help her tape a jumbo craft stick to the back of the cutout to make a puppet. Then write the word *apple* on the board. Help children name the beginning letter and listen for its sound as everyone says, "Apple."

Apple Trees

Here's an artistic apple tree that's just right for little hands! In advance, cut a large apple tree shape from tagboard for each child. Set out brown and green crayons and small bowls of glue to share. Each child will also need ten small red pom-poms. Invite each child to color his tree trunk brown and his leaves green. Help him dip each pom-pom into the glue and then press it onto the tree's leaves to resemble apples. Set the completed apple tree projects aside to dry. Later, help students count the apples on each tree. Yum—ten red apples!

As All Around!

Looking for more ways to increase *A* awareness? You've found it! Program a sheet of copy paper with a variety of large uppercase letters. Include several upper-case *A*s and space to write at the bottom of the page. Make a class supply of the sheet. Give each child a copy and a light-colored crayon. Invite her to circle each letter *A* she finds. For added practice, have her trace over each *A*. Then invite each child to use a pencil to practice writing a few *A*s at the bottom of the sheet.

Hunt for As

Build letter-identification skills with this super secret search around your classroom! In advance, write labels for a variety of classroom objects, making sure to include plenty whose names begin with the letter *A*. (Examples of *A* items include Raggedy Ann and Andy dolls, apples, plastic ants, and toy alligators.) After placing the labels with the items, have students walk around the room searching for items whose names begin with *A*. When a student finds an *A* item, instruct him to come whisper its name and location to you. Continue until each child has found at least one *A*. Awesome!

The A Game

Youngsters will enjoy helping an adorable ant think of short *A* words as you play this game together. To prepare, draw a simple ant on an index card and label it with the word *ant*. Have youngsters identify the ant; then talk about its beginning letter and sound. Hold up the ant card as you read the following rhyme to your group. Afterward, slowly "march" the ant behind your back as students name *A* words. Repeat as often as desired for "ant-tastic" fun!

"I just love *A* words," said the ant,
"Like apple, alligator, and avalanche."
How many *A* words can you say
Before the ant marches away?

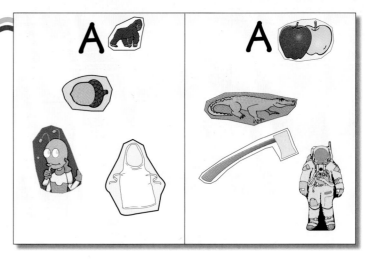

A Picture Wall

Picture letter *A* making long and short sounds on this decorative learning wall! In advance, cut out several pictures of objects whose names begin with the short *A* sound and several whose names begin with the long *A* sound. Display a length of bulletin board paper at student eye level. Visually divide the paper into two sections. In one section, write the letter *A*. Next to it, tape a picture of an object whose name begins with the long *A* sound (such as an ape). In the other section, write the letter *A* and tape a picture of an object whose name begins with the short *A* sound (such as an apple). To begin the activity, gather children around the display. Mention that both *ape* and *apple* begin with the letter *A*. Say the words and talk about the two different sounds of *A*. Then share the pictures with your little ones. Invite students to name each picture and notice either the long or short *A* sound. Then enlist student help to categorize the remaining pictures and tape them to the display. Continue with additional pictures throughout your *A* study.

Model As

It's time to practice forming the letter *A!* Give each child two regular craft sticks and a mini craft stick. Write a large uppercase *A* on the board, describing the strokes as you go. Next, model how to lay the sticks to resemble the letter *A*. Encourage each child to make an *A* with her sticks. Then, if desired, help each child glue her sticks together in the shape of an *A*. How many ways can you form an *A?*

A Is for Apple

Heighten print awareness with this twist on familiar apple sorting! In advance, program a number of index cards with the word *apple* written in red, yellow, or green marker and a matching apple illustration as shown. Place the cards and three small baskets in a center. Invite a child in this center to sort the apple cards by color, placing each into a different basket. When all the apples are sorted, have him compare the cards. Are all the words the same? Are all the pictures the same? Do they all have the short *A* sound? Looks like apple season to me!

Amazing *A* Moves

- Pretend to pick apples from a tree.
- Act like an alligator.
- March like an ant.
- Pretend to be an astronaut blasting into space.

A Snacks

- applesauce
- apple tarts
- apple slices
- apple juice
- animal crackers
- angel food cake

A Café

Stock your dramatic-play area with items to create an *A* café. Include empty food packages and play foods from the list above, such as animal cracker boxes; clean, empty apple juice boxes and plastic bottles; and plastic apples. Also set out materials for students to use to create signs, placemats, and menus.

The *A* Café Song
(sung to the tune of "Down by the Station")

Let's go out to eat
At the *A* café.
See the apple dumplings
Sitting in a row.

See the apple pies
Hot from the oven,
Yum, yum, yum, yum—
Let's all go!

A Parade

Plan an *A* parade with your youngsters! Pick and choose from the following costume and prop ideas. Then teach the provided song and let the marching begin!

Costumes

- aprons

- astronaut uniforms

- antlers

- angel wings

- *A* hats

  (Cut the center out of a paper plate, leaving a two-inch brim. Tie lengths of yarn on opposite sides of the hat.) Decorate the hat with things whose names begin with *A*.

Props

- apples

- toy alligators

- acorns

The *A* Parade Song

(sung to the tune of "When Johnny Comes Marching Home")

The *A*s are marching into town. Hooray! Hooray!
The *A*s are marching in a great big parade.
Some wear aprons and carry pies
Made from apples, my, oh, my.
Oh, we're so glad the *A*s could come today.

The *A*s are marching into town. Hooray! Hooray!
Some are tossing acorns as they come our way.
Some are crawling like ants on the ground;
Some are astronauts flying around.
Oh, we're so glad the *A*s could come today.

A Pattern
Use with "The Ants Go Marching" on page 4.

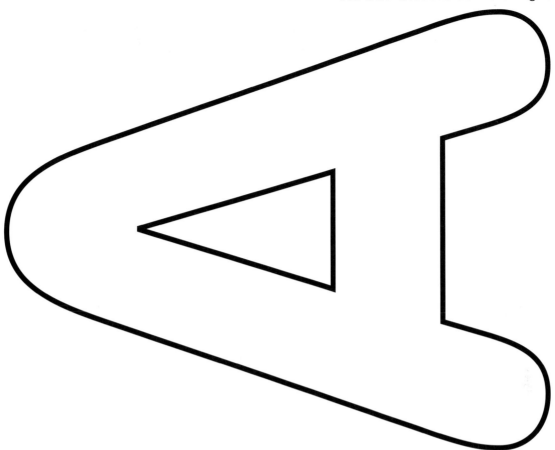

Apple Pattern
Use with "Apple Pal Puppets" on page 4.

The Letter B

Bubble Bs

The fun is bubblin' over with this activity, which builds phonemic awareness! In advance, combine thinned tempera paint and a small amount of dish-washing detergent in a bowl. To begin, give each child a white construction paper *B* cutout (pattern on page 15) and a straw. Have him use the straw to blow into the mixture until bubbles extend over the rim of the bowl. Direct him to quickly place the *B* pattern over the top of the bowl and hold it in place for a few seconds before removing it. As he does this, have him say the word *bubbles* and listen for the beginning /b/ sound. (If desired, repeat the procedure several times using different sizes of bowls and a variety of paint colors.)

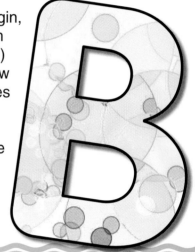

Bear Puppets

These "bear-y" special puppets are perfect to incor-porate into your letter activities for *B.* Make a brown construction paper copy of the bear pattern on page 15 for each student. Give each child a pattern, and help him cut it out and draw facial features on it. Next, direct him to spread glue on portions of the bear to represent its stomach, ears, and paws. Then have him sprinkle dried coffee grounds atop the glue. When the glue dries, shake off the excess coffee grounds. Then help each child tape a craft stick to the back of the bear for a handle. To complete the puppet, have each child give his bear puppet a name that begins with *B.* Then assist each child in writing the name on the craft stick.

Deep Blue Sea Bs

Crayons and paint team up to reveal a sea of *B*s with this activity. Place yellow crayons, white paper, thinned blue tempera paint, and wide paintbrushes at a center. Have each child use a crayon to write an uppercase and a lowercase *B* on provided paper. Then have her paint the entire page to showcase the letter. Wow! Swim-ming *B*s!

Where's the *B?*

Reinforce letter recognition with this fun game. While students are out of the room, hide a set of alphabet blocks in easy-to-spot places around the classroom. To begin, pair students and give each pair a grocery bag. Then challenge students to search for the hidden blocks. Each time a student pair finds a block, one partner names the letter on the block and the other partner places it in the bag. The first pair to find the *B* block announces, "We found *B!*" Then gather partners in a circle and invite the pair that found the *B* block to share it wit h the class. If desired, ask student volunteers to name words that begin with the /b/ sound.

Beanbag Toss

Any way you toss it, this activity is sure to be a hit! Use masking tape to form an uppercase and a lowercase *B* on the floor. Set up a beanbag toss by positioning a tape line on the floor a few feet from the letters. Invite a small group of children to the area. Challenge each youngster, in turn, to stand behind the tape line, say the sound *B* makes, and share a word that begins with that sound. Then have him attempt to toss the beanbag onto the letter. Finally, have him identify whether he hit (or nearly hit) the uppercase or lowercase *B*. When several youngsters demonstrate accurate tossing from this distance, provide a second line of tape that's farther away from the *B*s.

Bs in Print

This idea is just off the press and will help students recognize the letter *B* in a variety of fonts. On a sheet of poster board, use a marker to write an uppercase and a lowercase *B* in big block letters. Then, if desired, glue yarn around each letter for a tactile clue. Have each child search through old newspapers and magazines to find this letter. Have her cut out the letters and glue them on the matching uppercase or lowercase letter as shown.

What's in the Basket?

A tisket, a tasket, put *B*s in a basket! To prepare, collect three baskets with handles and stock the classroom with items that begin with the /b/ sound, such as balls, bears, bells, books, bottles, bows, and beanbags. At circle time, give each of three students a basket. Direct her to search the classroom for an item beginning with the /b/ sound (just like *basket*), place it in her basket, and return to the circle. When all three youngsters have returned to the circle, ask each one, in turn, to share her item. If the item begins with the /b/ sound, label it with a sticky note and display it on a table. If the item doesn't begin with the /b/ sound, assist the student in locating a /b/ item. Continue in this manner until each child has had a turn.

B Books

Shop for letter-sound awareness with a class book that features the letter *B*. To begin, write the letter *B* on the board. Say the name of the letter and its sound. Next, give each child a sheet of construction paper and have her write *B* on her paper. Then direct her to search through old catalogs and magazines, cut out pictures of items that begin with the /b/ sound, and glue them to her paper. Invite students to share their completed projects before compiling the pages into a class book.

B Animal Mural

Venture to the wild side as students create a mural featuring animals whose names begin with *B*. Gather a variety of books that contain pictures of animals that begin with *B*. During circle time, ask students to help you make a list of animals that begin with the /b/ sound, such as birds, bears, bugs, bees, beavers, bobcats, bunnies, baboons, and butterflies. Display pictures of the animals if possible. Then place the pictures at a center along with crayons and a length of bulletin board paper. During center time, have each student draw and label (or dictate if necessary) a picture of one of these animals on the paper. Post the completed mural for all to see.

Beautiful *B* Moves

- Fly like butterflies.
- Crawl like bugs.
- Bounce like a ball.
- Hop like a bunny.
- Buzz around like a bee.
- Pretend to row a boat or ride a bike.

B Snacks

- bread and butter with berry jam
- bear-shaped graham crackers
- berry or banana milk shakes
- bananas
- banana bread
- broccoli stalks with dip
- barbecue chips

B Café

Stock your dramatic-play area with items to create a *B* café. Include empty food packages and play foods from the list above along with items such as baker hats, baskets, plastic bowls, and a bell (for service). Also set out materials for students to use to create signs, placemats, and menus.

The *B* Café Song
(sung to the tune of "Yankee Doodle")

The *B* café is new in town
With *B* foods—what a treat.
Let's go down and check it out
And order food to eat.

Biscuits, butter, berry jam,
Burritos, and bean dip too.
Blueberries and banana bread
Baked fresh just for you.

B Parade

Plan a *B* parade with your youngsters! Pick and choose from the following costume and prop ideas. Then teach the provided song and let the marching begin!

Costumes

- baseball caps

- basketball jerseys

- butterfly wings

- ballerina tutus

- bonnets

- baby bibs

Props

- baskets

- balls and/or plastic bats

- toy banjos

- stuffed bears

- bubbles

- bells

- baby bottles

- books

The *B* Parade Song
(sung to the tune of "When Johnny Comes Marching Home")

The *B*s are marching into town. Hooray! Hooray!
The *B*s are marching in a great big *B* parade.
Some carry books; some carry bats.
Some wear bonnets or baseball caps.
Oh, we're so glad the *B*s could come today.

The *B*s are marching into town. Hooray! Hooray!
Some blow bubbles as they come our way.
Some play bells and banjos too.
Some carry bears that wear tutus.
Oh, we're so glad the *B*s could come today.

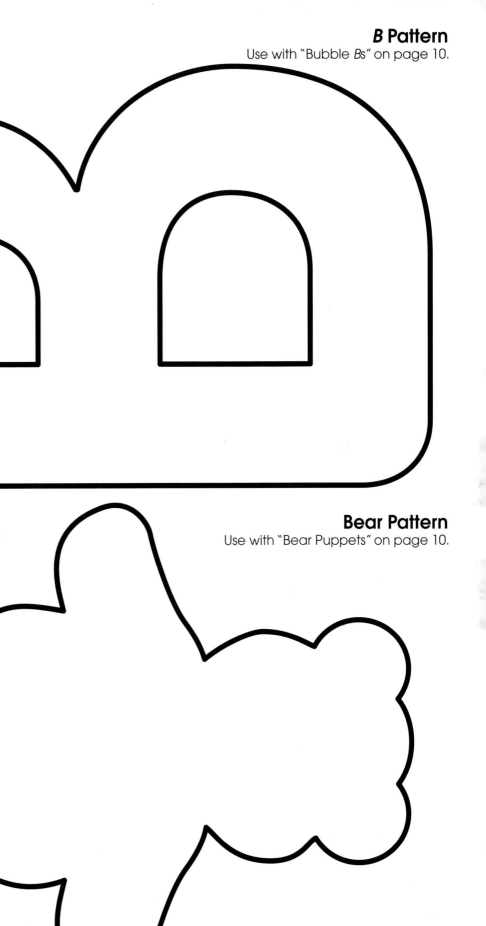

Bear Pattern
Use with "Bear Puppets" on page 10.

The Letter C

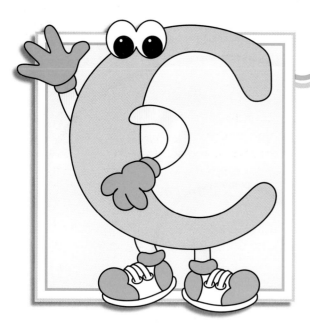

Cottony Cs

Combine phonemic awareness skills and fine-motor practice as youngsters learn about the letter *C*. Make a construction paper copy of the *C* pattern on page 21 for each child. Place cotton balls and a shallow bowl of glue at a center. First, discuss with youngsters the hard *C* sound and then guide them to name other words that begin with the same sound as *cotton.* Next, invite a small group to the center; give each child a copy of the letter and have him cut it out. Model for the group how to dip a cotton ball in glue and then stick it onto the letter. Have students repeat the process to complete their cottony creations.

Cactus Puppets

Teach youngsters about some of the parts of a cactus as they create these cute puppets. In advance, set out a shallow container of glue, cotton swabs, tissue paper scraps, and small pieces of spaghetti. Then give each child in a small group a green construction paper copy of the cactus pattern on page 21. Encourage each student to repeat the hard *C* sound as she cuts out her cactus. Explain to the group that the stem of the cactus holds water to help it live in hot, dry places. Then show students how to dip a cotton swab into glue, dab it onto a cactus, and then add pieces of spaghetti. Have each child repeat this process several times to make clusters of *spines* on the cactus. Explain that the spines protect the cactus from being eaten by animals. Then have each child roll several tissue paper flowers and glue them onto her cactus as shown. Explain that cactus flowers usually bloom for just a few days or less. After the project has dried, help each child glue a craft stick onto the back of it to make a puppet. Later, invite all your cute cacti to stand in a row and count off. One cactus, two cacti, three cacti, more!

Cute C Crafts

- Glue confetti on a paper crown.
- Create a construction paper caterpillar.
- Glue crunchy cereal onto a paper plate in the shape of the letter *C.*
- Use paint to make a fingerprint corn on the cob.
- Make a colorful construction paper cat.

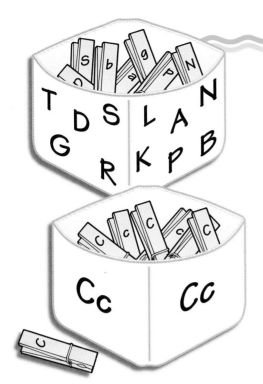

Cartons of Clothespins

Hit the target with letter recognition skills as youngsters play this small-group game. Gather two clean half-gallon milk cartons and a supply of wooden clothespins. Cut the top off of each milk carton. Use a permanent marker to label one carton with an uppercase and a lowercase *C* and the other carton with a variety of letters. Label half of the clothespins with the letter *C* and the remaining clothespins with different letters. Store the clothespins in a plastic container. Place the container on the floor beside the prepared cartons. Gather a small group of students, and invite one child to choose a clothespin and read the letter on it. Then have her stand near the cartons and try to drop her clothespin into the corresponding carton. Repeat the process until each child has had a turn. Then place the game at a center for continued letter recognition practice.

C Foods

Your little ones will be so proud when they make these yummy food booklets! First, make a blank booklet for each child by folding several sheets of white paper in half and stapling them together along the top as shown. To begin, write an uppercase and a lowercase *C* on the board and ask students to say the hard sound this letter makes. Then challenge youngsters to name foods that begin with this sound as you list their ideas under the letters. Next, give each child a booklet and have her write "*C* Foods" and her name on the cover; then have her decorate it as desired. Help each youngster write or dictate a word from the board on each booklet page. Then have her illustrate each word on the corresponding booklet page. To conclude, invite student pairs to read their booklets to each other.

Writing Wall

Students will be amazed that it's okay to write on the wall with this letter formation activity. In advance, line one wall with a long sheet of bulletin board paper, and place washable markers on the floor beneath the paper. Model for your group the correct way to write an uppercase and a lowercase *C*. Then invite a small group of students to practice writing the letter on the paper-lined wall. Continue in this manner with additional groups until each child has had a turn.

Colorful Cats

Reinforce the hard *C* sound as your youngsters practice sorting by color. Gather 20 index cards and label each of four cards with a different color word. Enlist students' help to draw a simple cat that matches the color word on each card. Then mix the cards and store them in a resealable plastic bag. At circle time, review the hard *C* sound at the beginning of the words *color* and *cat.* Then enlist students' help in sorting the cards by color word (or cat color). Place the bag of cards at a center for further color word practice.

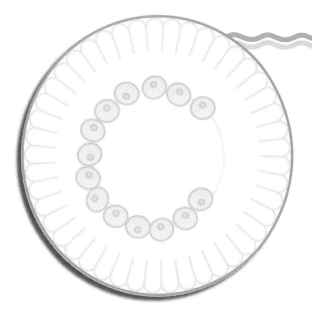

Count on Corn

Youngsters will crunch their way through this tasty counting and letter formation activity! Give each child a scoop of corn cereal on a paper plate. First, discuss the hard *C* sound students hear at the beginning of *corn* and *count.* Then have each youngster count his corn cereal and announce his total in turn. Next, ask each child to form a letter *C* with his corn cereal; then have him count the number of pieces used. Compare the results with the group. Then invite each child to munch his letter *C* one piece of cereal at a time. Yum!

Critter Cards

Use cute critters to reinforce the hard *C* sound as youngsters practice sorting skills. In advance, gather a set of animal stickers with pictures whose names begin with *C*. Then attach each one to a separate index card. At circle time, discuss the *C* sound and ask students to identify animals whose names begin with this sound. List their ideas on a chart. Then place the cards faceup in the middle of your group. One at a time, show students a prepared card and ask youngsters to name the animal. If the animal is on the list, place a check beside it. If it's not on the list, be sure to add it. Also ask student volunteers to draw on a card any animal not pictured on the cards but that is on the list. To review, show youngsters each card and have them name each animal, emphasizing the beginning sound. Then place the cards in a center and encourage students to sort the cards in several different ways (such as animals that do or do not have wings, animals that live on land or water, and animals that are wild or tame).

18

C Calisthenics

- Crawl like a caterpillar.
- Climb like a cat.
- Walk sideways like a crab.
- Pretend to be a cowboy on a horse.

C Snacks

- cupcakes
- cocoa
- corn chips
- corn muffins
- cookies
- cucumbers

C Café

Stock your dramatic-play area with items for youngsters to create a *C* café. For example, you might use chef hats, measuring cups, colanders, cupcake papers, and several toy foods from the list above. Also set out art materials for students to use to create signs, menus, and placemats for the café.

The *C* Café Song
(sung to the tune of "Jingle Bells")

C café,
C café,
Full of special treats.
Let's all go and have some lunch.
It's just down the street.

Cakes and crackers,
Cookies and cocoa.
Oh, what should I eat?
I just love the *C* café
With all of its *C* treats.

C Parade

Plan a *C* parade with your children! Use the dramatic-play ideas shown to provide costumes and props for youngsters as they sing and march in the parade.

Costumes

- clown hats
- cowboy hats, bandanas, and boots
- construction worker hats
- crowns
- capes
- coats

Props

- castanets
- clean combs
- cards
- plastic carrots
- stuffed cats
- cookbooks
- cotton balls
- caboose
- paper confetti

The *C* Parade Song
(sung to the tune "When Johnny Comes Marching Home")

The *C*s are marching into town. Hooray! Hooray!
The *C*s are marching in a great big *C* parade.
Some have cars and carry cats.
Some wear crowns or cowboy hats.
Oh, we're so glad the *C*s could come today.

The *C*s are marching into town. Hooray! Hooray!
They are playing castanets as they come our way.
Some are clowning all around.
Some throw confetti up and down.
Oh, we're so glad the *C*s could come today.

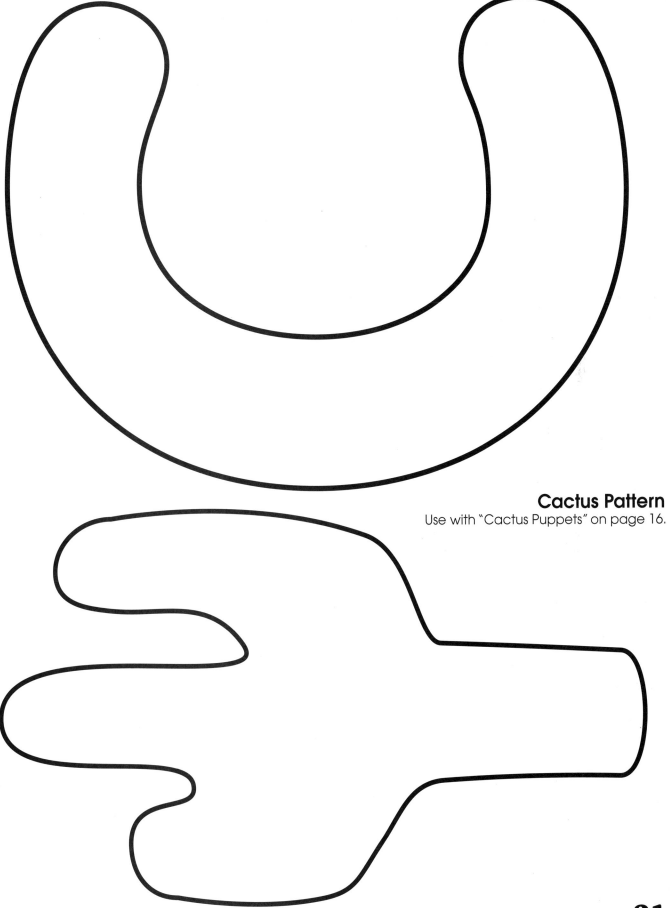

Cactus Pattern
Use with "Cactus Puppets" on page 16.

The Letter D

Dotted Ds

This delightful activity will have your youngsters seeing lots of dots as they learn about the letter *D!* Cut out a colorful construction paper copy of the *D* pattern on page 27 for each child. Display a cutout and have students say the letter and its sound. Then give each child a half sheet of colored dot stickers. Direct him to count as he attaches a predetermined number of dots to his cutout as desired.

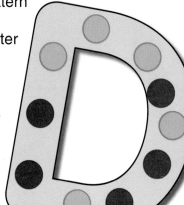

Dancing Doll Puppets

Combine phonemic awareness and fine-motor skills as youngsters create these darling doll puppets. To prepare, make a tagboard copy of one of the doll patterns on page 27 for each child and yourself. Cut out the finger holes on each doll. Place art materials and glue on a table for easy access by youngsters. To begin, write the words *dancing doll* on the board and talk about the beginning sound in each word. Next, invite students to use the art supplies to decorate their dolls. When the dolls are dry, have each child cut out her doll. Then show students how to position their fingers through the holes to make their puppets dance.

Door Decorations

Reinforce the /d/ sound as students enjoy making one or more of the following arts-and-crafts projects. No doubt they're perfect for displaying on your classroom door!
- Create doodle drawings.
- Make daisy prints from flower-shaped sponges.
- Make a collage of diamond shapes.
- Design a picture with colored sticker dots.
- Imagine and draw a new dog breed.
- Draw dinosaurs.

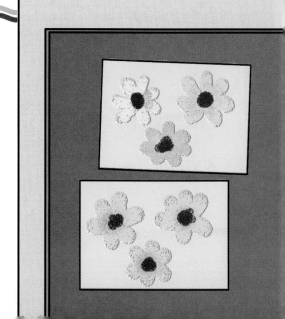

Dynamite Detectives!

Provide your little detectives with word recognition and writing skills with this small-group activity. In advance, label classroom objects including objects whose names begin with the letter *D,* such as a door, a desk, a doll, a drum, and dishes. Give each child in the group a magnifying glass (or a cutout of one) and a clipboard with paper and a pencil. Invite each child to search the classroom for words that begin with the letter *D.* Instruct him to copy each *D* word he finds onto his paper. Later, during group time, help youngsters read the words from their lists, emphasizing the beginning sound.

Dandy Book

This dandy book gives youngsters practice identifying pictures of items whose names begin with the /d/ sound. First, make a blank booklet for each child by folding several sheets of paper in half and stapling them together along the left side as shown. Discuss with students the /d/ sound; ask them to name words that begin with the sound. Give each child a booklet and help her write "My Letter *D* Book" and her name on the cover. Then ask her to draw on the cover a picture of something whose name begins with the /d/ sound. Have her cut out magazine pictures of things whose names begin with the /d/ sound and glue one on each page of her booklet. If desired, help her write the picture word on each page. Then have each child take her booklet home to share with family.

What's in a Name?

Youngsters will discover there are plenty of sounds in their names with this activity. During circle time have students say the letter *D* and its sound. Then ask a child to say his name out loud. Have the group help him decide whether he hears the /d/ sound in his name. If his name does have the /d/ sound, write it on a chart. Then have him use a marker to circle the letter. Repeat the process so that each child has a turn saying his name. When all of the uppercase and lowercase *D*s have been found, have your youngsters count the number of each that are circled.

Dirt Discoveries

Your little scientists will be amazed that they get to play in the dirt during this partner center activity! To prepare, gather two shallow pans, plastic scoops, plastic colanders, magnifying glasses, and two different types of soil. Place the items at a center. Discuss with youngsters the sound they hear at the beginning of the word *dirt.* Then, during center time, have each student place a scoop of each dirt sample in a separate pan and use a magnifying glass to investigate. Encourage partners to compare the similarities and differences in the two dirt samples.

Diamond Hunt

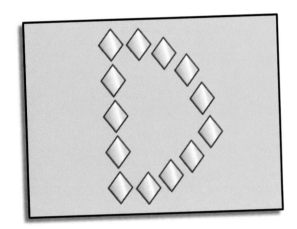

Extend your study of shapes to include this diamond *D!* Cut a supply of diamond shapes from foil or shiny wrapping paper and secretly hide them in the classroom while students are out of the room. At circle time write the letter *D* and talk about the /d/ sound. Show students a diamond shape and ask them to identify it. Tell them that while they were out you sprinkled diamond dust in the classroom and that diamonds may now be growing there. Invite students to search the classroom to find the diamonds. Then have each child arrange her diamonds on a sheet of construction paper to form a letter *D* and glue them in place. (Have extra diamonds available for youngsters who need them.) Display the completed projects on a bulletin board titled "Dazzling *D*s!"

Dozen Game

Count on this small-group game to provide dozens of ways to have fun! Gather four clean, foam egg cartons, a basket with 48 plastic eggs, and a large foam die. Ask youngsters to name the sound they hear at the beginning of *dozen, dice,* and *dots.* Then discuss how many are in a dozen. To play the game, give each of four students a carton and set the basket of eggs nearby. Have the first player roll the die and count the number of dots. Then have her take the corresponding number of eggs from the basket and place them in her carton. Repeat the process with each player. Continue until one child has filled her carton. Have the child count her eggs out loud and say, "Twelve makes one dozen!"

Delightful *D* Moves

- Dance to the beat of a drum.
- Waddle like a duck.
- Do dog tricks such as sitting, rolling over, and lying down.
- Stomp and roar like a dinosaur.
- Pretend to dig in the dirt.

D Snacks

- doughnuts
- dill pickles
- dip and vegetables
- dessert

D Café

Stock your dramatic-play area with items for youngsters to create a *D* café. Include dishes, empty dairy containers, dishpans, and several play foods from the list above. Also set out materials for students to use to create signs, menus, and placemats.

The *D* Café Song
(sung to the tune of "Yankee Doodle")

Let's go to the *D* café
To get a bite to eat.
Let's go to the *D* café;
It's where everybody meets.

Yummy donuts, dips, and dates,
Dill pickles and desserts too,
Even devil's food cake
Baked daily just for you.

D Parade

Plan a *D* parade with youngsters! Pick and choose from the following costume and prop ideas. Then teach the provided song and let the marching begin!

Costumes

- dancing shoes
- fancy dresses
- detective gear
- diver's goggles
- doctor outfits
- dotted scarves

Props

- dusters and dustpans
- dolls
- dump trucks
- drums
- stuffed dogs and/or ducks
- toy dinosaurs

The *D* Parade Song
(sung to the tune "When Johnny Comes Marching Home")

The *D*s are marching into town. Hooray! Hooray!
The *D*s are marching in a great big *D* parade.
Some play drums and dance around.
Some throw dollars on the ground.
Oh, we're so glad the *D*s could come today.

The *D*s are marching into town. Hooray! Hooray!
Some are dressed like dolls as they come our way.
Some hold ducks and dinosaurs.
Some wear diamonds and dust the floor.
Oh, we're so glad the *D*s could come today.

D Pattern
Use with "Dotted *D*s" on page 22.

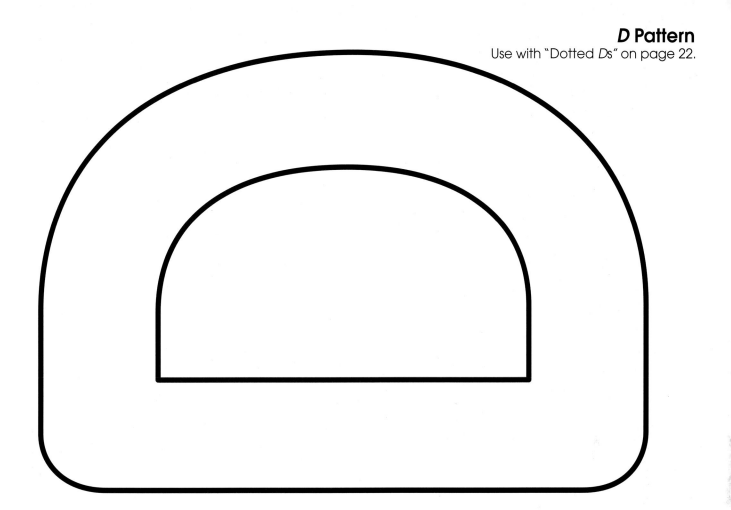

Doll Pattern
Use with "Dancing Doll Puppets" on page 22.

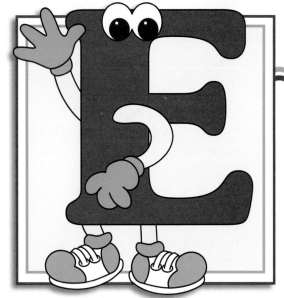

The Letter E

Embellishing Es

Youngsters are sure to remember the name of letter *E* with this "egg-stra" special learning opportunity! Enlarge the *E* pattern on page 33. Then make a copy on white construction paper for each student. To begin, invite one or more children to your art table. Give each child a pattern. Encourage her to trace the letter with her finger while she says its name. Then have her place the paper in a shallow pan. Next, dip a plastic egg in tempera paint and place it on the paper. Encourage each youngster to roll the egg across the paper by gently tilting the pan. When a desired effect is achieved, remove the paper and allow time for the paint to dry. Have students cut out their letters. Then post the letters in the classroom to make an "egg-cellent" display!

Egghead Puppets

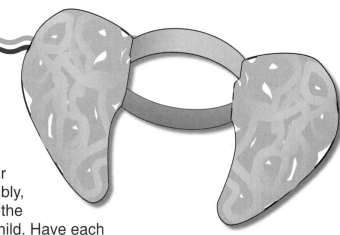

What has two eyes, a nose, and a white shell? These playful egghead puppets! Give each child a white construction paper copy of the egg pattern on page 33 and have her cut it out. Then have her cut colorful construction paper features and glue them to the egg to resemble a face. Help each youngster tape a jumbo craft stick to the back of the project to make a puppet. Allow time for the glue to dry. Then have each youngster use the puppet for dramatic play or as a companion when reviewing the letter *E* and its sounds.

Elephant Ears

Little ones will be all ears when they listen for the short *E* sound while wearing these playful headbands! To begin, give each child a 12" x 18" sheet of white construction paper and have him fingerpaint the paper gray. When the paint is dry, cut two elephant ear shapes from the paper. To aid in the headband assembly, fold a tab on the inside edge of each ear. Then staple the tabs to opposite sides of a headband sized to fit the child. Have each child don his headband. Then say a word. If the word begins with the short *E* sound as in *elephant,* encourage the children to stand up and trumpet like an elephant. If the word does not begin with the short *E* sound, encourage them to stay seated. This is an activity your little elephants will never forget!

Little Elf
(sung to the tune of "Are You Sleeping")

Little elf, little elf,
What do you see that starts with *E?*
[She] sees an [envelope].
[She] sees an [envelope].
We agree;
It starts with *E!*

What Do You See?

An elf on an *E* quest is the focus of this fun tune and activity! Gather or make several picture cards that show items with names that begin with the short E sound, such as an envelope, a train engine, an egg, an elf, an elephant, and an elbow. Place the cards picture side up on a tabletop. To begin, choose a child to be the elf. Lead youngsters in singing the song, pausing after the second line to invite the child to choose a card from the table. Then continue singing the song, substituting the name of the object in lines three and four. Continue in a similar fashion, choosing a new child to be the elf for each repetition.

Es in an Envelope

What would be the best holder for the *E*s found during this letter search? Why, an envelope, of course! Place a sheet of colorful poster board on a tabletop. To begin, give each child an envelope labeled with an uppercase and a lowercase *E.* Encourage each child to cut *E*s from old magazines and place them in his envelope. After each student has found several *E*s, encourage him to remove them from the envelope and glue them to the poster board. Then display this *E* poster in your classroom.

Everything Es

Supply youngsters with a variety of props, and they can make *E*s aplenty! Place in a container a variety of items conducive to forming an uppercase *E,* such as craft sticks, blunt-end toothpicks, penne pasta, unsharpened pencils, and construction paper strips. Then place the container at a table. Invite children to the table and encourage them to choose supplies and manipulate them to form several *E*s on the tabletop. After observing each child's work, invite her to whisper the short *E* sound in your ear before placing the supplies back in the container.

Egg Match

Youngsters delight in matching these lovely eggs! Gather a variety of wallpaper samples and cut two egg shapes from each one. For each matching pair, write an uppercase *E* on the back of one egg and a lowercase *E* on the back of the other. Place the eggs in a container. Then place the container in a center. Invite up to two students to the center. Encourage youngsters to say the word *egg* as they carefully listen for the short *E* sound. Then have them dump out the container of eggs and flip them over so the wallpaper patterns are facing up. Encourage the students to take turns matching each egg to its identical twin. When all the eggs have been matched, have the youngsters flip the eggs back over. Each matching pair shows an uppercase and a lowercase *E.* It's a match!

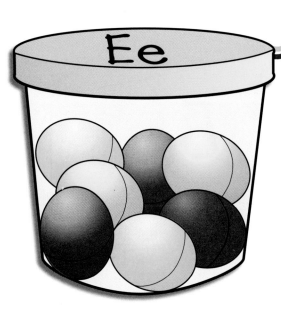

"Egg-stimating"

Five? Eight? Twenty? Keep your little ones guessing with this *E*-themed estimation activity. Use a permanent marker to write an uppercase and a lowercase *E* on the lid of a transparent plastic container. Then place several plastic eggs in the container. To begin, invite students to guess how many eggs are in the container. If desired, have each child write his guess on a sticky note and post it in a designated location. Then count the eggs orally as a class for youngsters to evaluate their predictions. If desired, repeat the activity with a different number of eggs.

Egg Carton Numbers

Students shake their way to number knowledge with this egg carton game! Clean and sanitize a foam egg carton. Then use a permanent marker to write a different numeral from 1 to 12 on the inside of each egg cup. Invite a small group of children to a table and give a child the egg carton. Have the student place a plastic bottle cap in the carton and then close the lid. Then encourage the child to shake the carton while you lead the students in the chant provided. When the chant is finished, encourage the child to open the container and name the number under the bottle cap. Continue in the same way until each child has had a turn to shake the egg carton.

The Egg Carton Shake

Shake it to the left.
Shake it to the right.
Shake it up and down.
Shake with all your might.

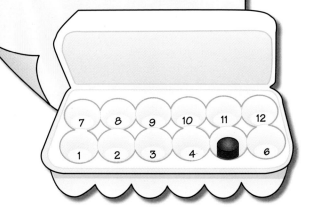

E Exercises

- Walk like an elephant.
- Wiggle your elbows.
- Roll like an egg.
- Glide up and down like an elevator.
- Move like a train engine.
- Sway like an evergreen tree.

E Snacks

- hard-boiled eggs
- egg rolls
- enchiladas
- elephant ears

E Café

Stock your dramatic-play area with items to create an *E* café. Include cleaned and sanitized egg cartons, plastic eggs, egg baskets, and egg cups. Add fried eggs or scrambled eggs made from craft foam and a frying pan with a spatula. Also set out materials for students to use to create signs, placemats, and menus.

The *E* Café Song
(sung to the tune of "She'll Be Comin' Round the Mountain")

Oh, welcome to our tasty *E* café!
Oh yes, welcome to our tasty *E* café!
We'll make your egg any way,
And it's guaranteed Grade A!
Oh yes, welcome to our tasty *E* café!

Oh, welcome to our tasty *E* café!
Oh yes, welcome to our tasty *E* café!
We have eggs scrambled and fried,
Poached, hard-boiled, even dyed!
Oh yes, welcome to our tasty *E* café!

31

E Parade

Plan an *E* parade with your youngsters! Pick and choose from the following costume and prop ideas. Then teach the provided song and let the marching begin!

Costumes

- engineer hats

- exercise-related clothing such as sweatshirts, headbands, and wristbands

- elephant ears (see "Elephant Ears" on page 28)

- elf hat headbands (Staple a green construction paper triangle to a headband. Glue a pom-pom to the top of the triangle.)

Props

- stuffed elephants

- artificial evergreens

- baskets filled with plastic eggs

- large manila envelopes decorated with the letter *E*

- egg shakers (Place a spoonful of rice in a plastic egg. Then reinforce the seam with masking tape.)

The *E* Parade Song
(sung to the tune of "When Johnny Comes Marching Home")

The *E*s are marching into town. Hooray! Hooray!
The *E*s are marching in a great big *E* parade!
There are evergreens we wave around
And eggs that make a nice rattling sound.
Oh, we're so glad the *E*s could come today.

The *E*s are marching into town. Hooray! Hooray!
The *E*s are marching in a great big *E* parade!
I see an elf in a fun disguise
And people ready to exercise.
Oh, we're so glad the *E*s could come today.

E Pattern

Use with "Embellishing *E*s" on page 28.

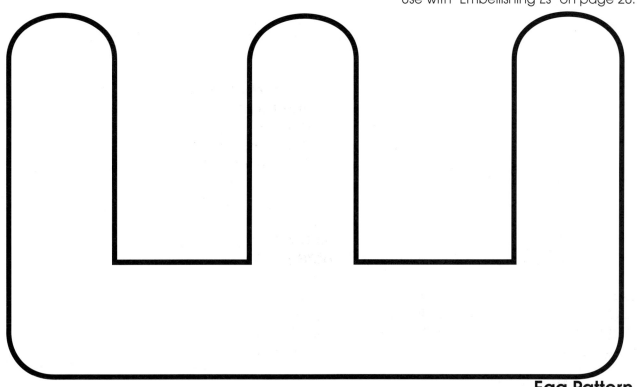

Egg Pattern

Use with "Egghead Puppets" on page 28.

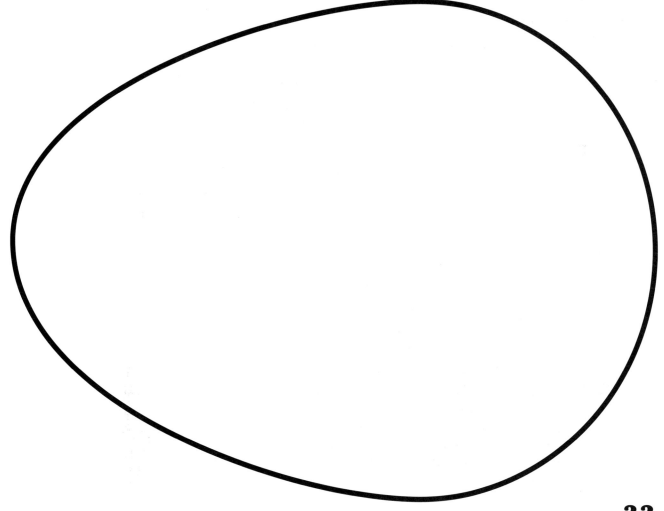

33

The Letter F

Fantastic *F*s

When students finish this *F* project there will be plenty of phonemic awareness practice at hand! In a designated area, place an assortment of rubber stamps depicting items that begin with the /f/ sound, such as a fox, five, four, a fish, a flower, or a frog. Also supply colorful stamp pads and a class supply of construction paper *F* cutouts from the pattern on page 39. To decorate a shape, each child stamps an assortment of pictures on his *F* cutout. When he's finished, have him name each picture and verify the beginning sound. *Fish* starts with the /f/ sound. That's fantastic!

Fish Puppet

Just add water—pretend, of course—when these puppets are complete, and students will make a splash with the letter *F!* Provide each child with a copy of the fish pattern (page 39), a small paper lunch bag, crayons, glue, and assorted craft supplies. To make a fish, have each child write the letter *F* on her fish pattern and say the /f/ sound. Then have her color the fish and decorate it as desired. Finally, have her glue the fish to the paper bag so that the fish's mouth points toward the closed end of the bag. When the glue dries, she simply puts her hand inside the bag and sets the fish in motion. For added fun, hang blue crepe paper streamers from a puppet stage to make a water scene for the puppets to swim in.

More *F* Art Ideas

Emphasize the /f/ sound as students enjoy one or more of these fun-filled arts-and-crafts projects.
- Decorate frames with feathers.
- Fingerpaint.
- Make finger puppets from felt.
- Turn fingerprints into fish, frogs, or flowers.

Finding *Fs*

This hands-on search helps students recognize the /f/ sound. Gather five objects that begin with the /f/ sound, such as felt, a feather, a fork, a toy fish, and a silk flower. Also gather five small items that begin with a sound or sounds other than /f/. Randomly place the items in your circle area. Then have students take turns selecting items that begin with the /f/ sound. Be sure to involve all your students in naming each selected item and saying its beginning sound. With a quick change of objects, this activity can be used again and again.

Fee! Fie! Foe! Fum!

The /f/ sound takes center stage in this fun verse! Say the following verse aloud to your students.
Fee! Fie! Foe! Fum!
Freddy found four [floating feathers].
Have students repeat the verse and listen for the beginning /f/ sound. On repeated readings, change the words *floating feathers* to other beginning /f/ sound word pairs, such as *funny fish* or *fancy fiddles.* Occasionally exchange a pair of words for words that don't begin with *F.* Students will be eager to point out your mistake. When the verse is familiar, encourage students to substitute their own choices of words that begin with *F.* Fee! Fie! Foe! Fum! That's a lot of /f/ sound fun!

Fishing for *Fs*

Your students will think this letter recognition activity is a real catch! Make ten copies of the fish pattern (page 39) on colorful construction paper. Cut out the fish; then attach a paper clip to the tail of each one. Label each of five fish with the letter *F.* Label the remaining fish with other familiar letters. Prepare a simple fishing pole by tying a magnet to one end of a length of string and then tying the free end of the string to a wooden dowel or cardboard tube. Arrange the fish on the floor and gather a small group of students. To play, a student uses the pole to catch a fish; then she identifies the letter on it. If the letter is an *F,* she keeps the fish. If it is not an *F,* she puts the fish back. Have students take turns until all the *F* fish have been caught.

F Book

Letter-sound recognition pairs perfectly with these student-made *F* books. For each child, fold three sheets of white paper and staple along the fold. Label the front of each book with the child's name and the title "My Letter *F* Book." To fill each page, a student draws a picture of an item that begins with *F*. Then she writes the letter *F* on the page. She continues with different *F* pictures until the book is full. Feature students' books during storytime for some added *F* practice.

F Measurement

Measurement takes on a fascinating new focus in this activity. In advance, create a chart like the one shown and make a copy for each pair of students. Also gather manipulatives whose names begin with *F* that students could use as nonstandard measurement tools (such as feathers or forks) and place each set in a different container. Show students each manipulative and then ask them to name each item and identify its beginning sound. Next, pair students and give each pair a copy of the chart and a set of manipulatives. Have one partner draw a picture of the manipulative on the back of the paper. Then have the pair move around the room from one pictured object to another, determining the length of each object by measuring it with the manipulatives. After the pair has measured each item, have one partner write the number on the chart.

For added fun, gather students and challenge them to measure the distance to a predetermined location in feet—student feet, that is! Have each child walk heel to toe to determine the distance.

Fish Habitat

Nonfiction books provide the background students need to help you establish a fish habitat in the classroom. Share facts about fish and their surroundings and then help students compile a list of items needed to keep a fish happy and comfortable. If possible, plan an outing for students to purchase the items from a pet store, or ask parents and students to contribute items from the list. After all the items are collected, introduce a fish to the new classroom environment. Give students a chance to name the class fish—with a name that begins with *F*, of course! Post a sign near the fishbowl with the fish's name for added reinforcement of the letter *F*.

Fancy *F* Moves

- Pretend to fly like a fairy.
- Float like a feather.
- Make funny faces.
- Pretend to be a flying fish.
- Fall like fall leaves.
- Pretend to fight a fire.

F Snacks

- fig cookies
- fruit cups
- fish-shaped crackers
- french fries
- fruit with fudge fondue

F Café

Stock your dramatic-play area with items to create an F café. Include empty food packages and play foods from the list above along with items such as funnels, fancy napkins and tablecloths, silk flowers, and plastic forks. Also set out materials for students to use to create signs, placemats, and menus.

The *F* Café Song
(sung to the tune of "Are You Sleeping?")

F café, *F* café—
Special treats, good to eat.
Fruit and fondue,
Fish and french fries,
Special treats, good to eat.

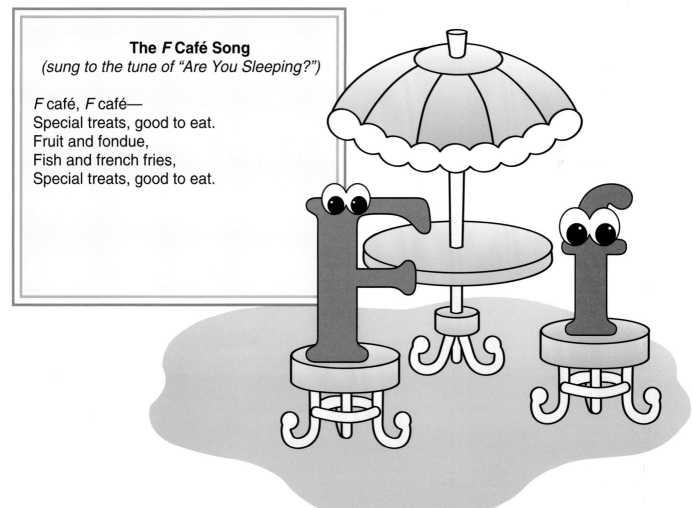

F Parade

Plan an *F* parade with your youngsters! Pick and choose from the following costume and prop ideas. Then teach the provided song and let the marching begin!

Costumes

- firefighter hats and coats

- fairy dresses and wings

- fishing hats and boots

- football uniforms and helmets

- fur or feather headbands

Props

- fans

- feathers

- flutes

- flags

- flowers

- fossils

- footballs

- funnels

- toy fish

The *F* Parade Song
*(sung to the tune of
"When Johnny Comes Marching Home")*

The *F*s are marching into town. Hooray! Hooray!
The *F*s are marching in a great big *F* parade.
Some ride fire trucks; some ride floats.
Some wear fancy flannel coats.
Oh, we're so glad the *F*s could come today.

The *F*s are marching into town. Hooray! Hooray!
Some are throwing feathers as they come our way.
Some play fiddles, and some play flutes.
Some wear fishing hats and boots.
Oh, we're so glad the *F*s could come today.

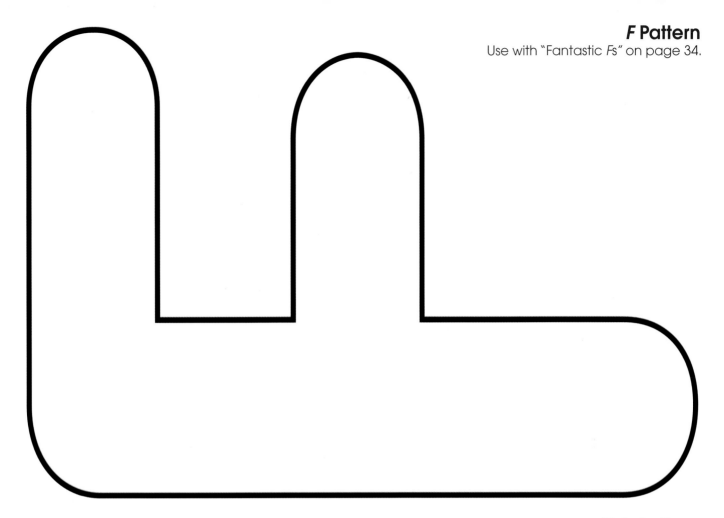

F Pattern
Use with "Fantastic Fs" on page 34.

Fish Pattern
Use with "Fish Puppet" on page 34 and "Fishing for Fs" on page 35.

The Letter G

Glittering Gs

This letter *G* activity is golden! Each child will need a construction paper copy of the *G* pattern on page 45, access to old paintbrushes, a shallow bowl of glue, scissors, and gold glitter. Discuss the letter *G* and encourage students to say the beginning sound they hear in *gold.* Next, have each child brush glue on her *G* pattern. Then have her sprinkle glitter on it. When the glue is dry, have her shake off the excess glitter and cut out her golden letter!

Galloping Goat Puppets

Clip-clop, clip-clop. All your little kids will enjoy galloping this goat puppet through your letter *G* activities! Make a construction paper copy of the goat pattern on page 45 for each child. During circle time, write the word *goat* on a chart and point out the letter and sound correlation. Give each child a copy of the goat pattern and have him color and cut it out. Then have him tape a craft stick to the back of his goat to make a puppet. Then invite students to pretend to make their puppets gallop as they say the /g/ sound.

Great Art Activities for G!

- Use gold, green, or gray paint to make a giant *G.*
- Use gold and green tissue paper squares to make a *G.*
- Tint glue with green food coloring and use it to write a large *G.*
- Use glue to squirt a design on construction paper; then sprinkle gold or green glitter on it.

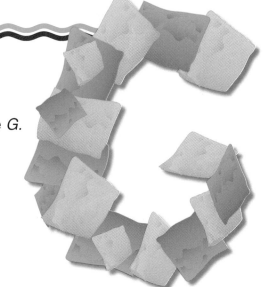

Green Gs

Little ones will glow with pride when they complete this letter-formation activity. In advance, write a large uppercase and a large lowercase *G* on the top half of a sheet of paper. Copy it to make a class supply. Model for youngsters how to write the letter on a chart or chalkboard. Then give each child a copy of the prepared sheet and ask her to trace the uppercase and lowercase letters with a green crayon or marker. Guide her to write one row of uppercase letters and one row of lowercase letters. Then invite her to place a green sticker above her best-written letter in each row. Display students' work on a board titled "Great Green *G*s!"

Great Stories

Use story books to give youngsters practice identifying the initial consonant *G* in words. Gather several books that feature *G*, such as *Go, Dog, Go!* by P. D. Eastman or *The Three Billy Goats Gruff*. Read one of the selections to the class. Next, review each page and help students find words that begin with the letter *G*. Then place the book at a center. When youngsters visit the center, challenge them to find and count words that begin with letter *G* in each story.

The goat ———
————
————

The green grass
————
————

Picture the Goal

Identifying the beginning hard *G* sound in picture words is the goal in this activity. To prepare, draw a soccer goal on a large sheet of bulletin board paper and cut out a class supply of four-inch white circles to resemble soccer balls. Discuss the beginning hard *G* sound of *goal* with students and help them name other words that begin with the same sound. Then have each child cut out a magazine picture that begins with the /g/ sound; have him glue it onto a ball. Help each little kicker make a goal by attaching his ball inside the soccer goal. Then review the picture words with the class, emphasizing the hard *G* sound.

Gumball Count

Great gumballs! Count on this activity to help youngsters practice beginning math and oral language skills. To prepare, draw a large gumball machine on construction paper; also cut out a supply of construction paper gumballs. Gather your group and discuss the hard *G* sound they hear in *gumballs.* Then use tape to attach several gumballs to the machine, and help students count them out loud. Next, lead your group in stating aloud the number counted, such as "three gumballs." Add several gumballs and lead youngsters in counting and stating the result again. Then take away several gumballs and lead the group in counting again. Repeat the activity several times to practice counting and beginning addition and subtraction skills. Then put the activity at a center to give each child an opportunity to count the gumballs!

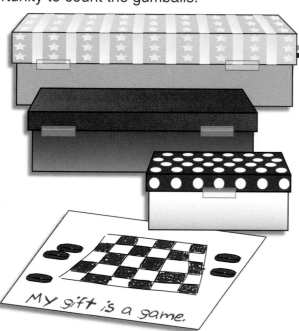

Gifts Galore!

Youngsters size up the gifts at this sequencing and writing center. Gather several different-size gift boxes and tape each one closed. Place the boxes at a center along with crayons and plain paper. As each child visits the center, ask her to sequence the boxes by size. Next, challenge her to think of a gift that begins with the hard *G* sound and draw it on a sheet of paper. Then help her write or dictate a sentence describing her gift. After each child has completed a page, combine the pages together to make a class book titled "Great Gifts Galore!"

Grrreat Animals!

Take advantage of students' love of animals to make the *G* letter-sound connection. Ask youngsters to name animals whose names begin with the letter *G,* such as goat, gorilla, goose, goldfish, grizzly bear, and grasshopper. Record students' ideas on a chart. Next, challenge youngsters to list colors that begin with the /g/ sound (green, gray, gold) and record them on the chart. Give each child a sheet of white paper and help him write or dictate a sentence using one animal and one color from the list. Then have him illustrate his sentence. Staple the students' completed pages together along with a cover to make a class book. After sharing it with the class, place it in the book center for all to enjoy!

Great G Moves

- Gallop like a goat or a horse.
- Hop like a grasshopper.
- Pretend to be a garbage collector lifting a heavy can.
- Flap your wings like a goose.
- Pretend to kick a goal.

G Snacks

- grape juice
- graham crackers
- granola cereal
- green beans
- garlic bread

G Café

Stock your dramatic-play area with items to create a *G* café. Include empty food containers from the grocery store, a plastic pitcher for grape juice, and play foods from the list above. Also set out materials for your students to use to create signs, placemats, and menus.

The *G* Café Song
(sung to the tune of "Yankee Doodle")

The *G* café is new in town!
The *G* foods are a treat.
Let's go down and check it out
And order food to eat.

Garlic bread and green beans,
Graham crackers too,
Grape juice and goulash—
They're waiting just for you.

G Parade

Plan a *G* parade with youngsters! Pick and choose from the following costume and prop ideas. Then teach the provided song and let the marching begin!

Costumes

- garden gloves

- glasses

- golf attire

- green clothing such as hats and vests

- galoshes

- fancy gowns

- goggles

- glitter headbands
  (Use green or gold glitter glue to decorate a construction paper headband.)

Props

- toy guitars

- toy golf clubs

- stuffed gorillas and/or goats

- garbage can lids

The *G* Parade Song
(sung to the tune "When Johnny Comes Marching Home")

The *G*s are marching into town. Hooray! Hooray!
The *G*s are marching in a great big *G* parade.
Some ride goats; some ride giraffes.
Some toss gumballs as they pass.
Oh, we're so glad the *G*s could come today.

The *G*s are marching into town. Hooray! Hooray!
They're playing guitars as they come our way.
Some wear gold gloves on their hands.
Some dance to a grasshopper band.
Oh, we're so glad the *G*s could come today.

G Pattern
Use with "Glittering *G*s" on page 40.

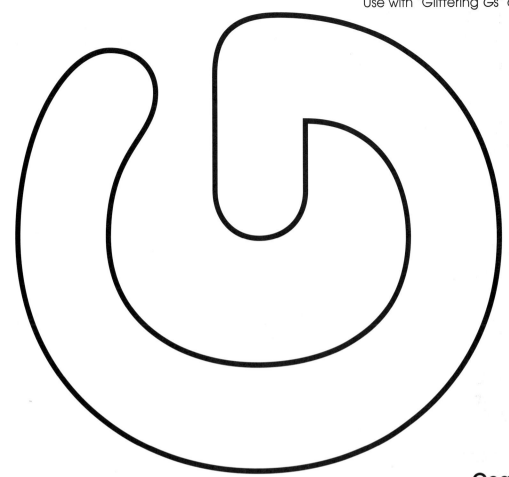

Goat Pattern
Use with "Galloping Goat Puppets" on page 40.

45

The Letter H

"Heart-y" Hs

Phonemic awareness is a heartbeat away with this letter *H* project. To prepare, gather heart stamps, ink pads, and a collection of heart-shaped stickers. Give each child a white construction paper copy of the *H* pattern on page 51. Instruct him to cut out the *H.* Then have him stamp hearts on his cutout or attach stickers to it. Each time he makes a print or adds a sticker, have him say the /h/ sound.

Stick Houses

Build a foundation for the letter *H* with this simple idea. Give each child a tagboard copy of the house pattern on page 51 and a supply of craft sticks. Have her glue sticks to the house shape as she desires. While students are working, discuss that the words *house* and *home* begin with *H.* When the glue is dry, invite each child to use markers to add details to her house. Display the houses on a bulletin board in the formation of an H-shaped neighborhood. Home, sweet home!

Holey Hearts

Little ones get language and fine-motor practice when they use a hole puncher to create these holey hearts. To prepare, cut a large construction paper heart for each child. Place the cutouts and several hole punchers at a center. Have each child who visits the center punch holes around the edge of his cutout. As he punches, encourage him to name different objects that begin with the letter *H.* When the child is finished punching holes, have him glue his heart to a light-colored sheet of construction paper to show off his beautifully hole-punched heart. *Horse, house, heart!*

46

Hat Memory Game

Grab some hats for this uppercase and lowercase *H* matching game! Collect or borrow ten hats. Label five index cards with uppercase *H*s and five index cards with lowercase *H*s. Attach each card to the inside of a different hat and then position the hats on a table. Invite a pair of children to play the game. In turn, have a child choose two hats. Instruct her to look at the *H*s inside the hats. If the two letters are an uppercase and lowercase *H* pair, she keeps the hats. If the *H*s inside each hat are the same, she returns them to the pile. Play continues until five pairs have been made. Hats off to the letter *H!*

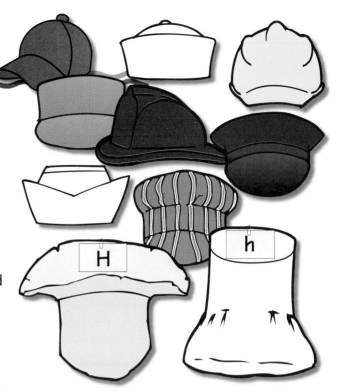

H Word Opposites

Focus on opposites with this easy activity. In turn, say each *H* word listed below and have students name its opposite. For each correct response, invite little ones to say, "Hooray!"

light

heavy

- high (low)
- hot (cold)
- heavy (light)
- hard (soft)
- half (whole)
- happy (sad)

Heart Puzzles

Youngsters are eager to put this broken heart back together! Cut a large heart from red craft foam. Use a permanent marker to write the word *heart* across it; then underline the letter *H.* Puzzle-cut the heart to make four or five pieces. Place the puzzle pieces at a center. Have each child arrange the pieces to make a heart. Then instruct him to use his finger to trace over the underlined letter. Before leaving the center, have him mix the puzzle pieces to ready the center for the next child. Aah, a happy, mended heart!

H Word Song

This idea and little ditty encourages youngsters to think of lots of words that begin with the letter *H*. Write the song shown on chart paper, leaving blanks where indicated. Laminate the chart. Use a dry-erase marker to fill in the *H* words shown. Then teach students the song. After singing the song several times, have youngsters brainstorm a list of other *H* words. Encourage students to help you use their words to create new verses for the song.

(sung to the tune of "The Farmer in the Dell")

A [horse] and a [hen],
A [hammer] and a [hat]—
They all begin with *H*.
Now what do you think of that?

H Stories

Head to the library to look for popular children's books and folktales that have *H* words in them! As you read the stories to students, emphasize the *H* words you come across. Have youngsters give you a thumbs-up every time they hear a word that begins with the letter *H*. Easy!

Healthy Is an H Word!

Use this idea to identify the letter *H* and promote healthy habits at the same time! Write "Healthy Habits" on a chart. Read the words and ask students to tell you with which letter each word starts. Then invite youngsters to brainstorm a list of habits that can help keep their bodies healthy. Write students' responses on the chart. Review the list, encouraging little ones to include the healthy habits in their daily routines. Then, in turn, invite youngsters to use a marker and circle the *H*s on the chart.

Healthy Habits
Brush your teeth
Eat healthy foods.
Keep your body clean.
Cover your mouth when you cough or sneeze.
Get plenty of rest each night.
Exercise each day.
Wash your hands.
Wear a helmet while riding a bike.

48

Happy *H* Moves

- Pretend to hammer.
- Hop like a hare.
- Pretend to hike up a hill.
- Hiss like a snake.
- Hug a friend.
- Pretend to get stuck in honey.

H Snacks

- hot dogs
- hamburgers
- heart-shaped cookies
- honeydew slices
- ham
- honey

H Café

Stock your dramatic-play area with items to create an H café. Include empty food packages and play foods from the list above, along with chefs' hats. Also set out materials for students to use to create signs, placemats, and menus.

The *H* Café Song
(sung to the tune of "Down by the Station")

Let's go out to eat
At the *H* café.
We'll see the little hot dogs
All in a row.

They have hamburgers
And heart cookies too.
Yum, yum, yum, yum—
Now off we go!

H Parade

Plan an *H* parade with your youngsters! Pick and choose from the following costume and prop ideas. Then teach the provided song and let the marching begin!

Costumes

- hats

- horse tails

- halos

Props

- play hammers

- large plastic hoops

- pretend hot dogs

- toy helicopters

- horns

- small hobby horses

- hairbrushes

- harps

- heart headbands
  (Write an *H* on several heart cutouts. Then glue each heart onto a headband.)

The *H* Parade Song

Give each child a small supply of small heart cutouts. Have her write an *H* on each cutout. During the parade, have youngsters pass out their hearts to spectators.

(sung to the tune of "When Johnny Comes Marching Home")

The *H*s are marching into town. Hooray! Hooray!
The *H*s are marching in a great big *H* parade.
Some ride horses; some wave hands.
Some blow horns in a big band.
Oh, we're so glad the *H*s could come today.

The *H*s are marching into town. Hooray! Hooray!
They pass out *H* hearts as they come our way.
Some wear hats covered with hearts.
Some wear halos and play their harps.
Oh, we're so glad the *H*s could come today.

50

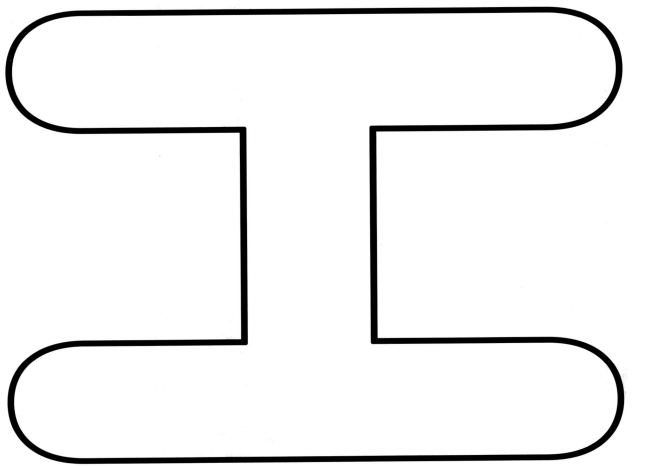

House Pattern
Use with "Stick Houses" on page 46.

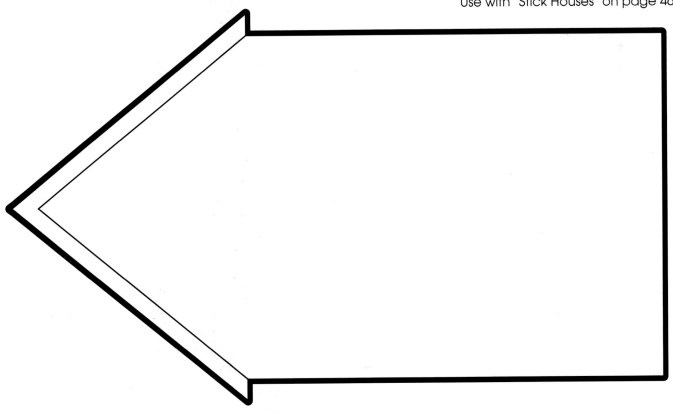

The Letter *I*

I Is for *Insect*

Interesting insects and the letter *I* come together with this simple craft that reinforces letter-sound correspondence. Make a copy of the *I* pattern on page 57 for each child and obtain an assortment of colorful insect stickers. Write the word *insect* on the board and point out the letter-sound connection. Have each child use her finger to trace the *I* on her paper as she says the short *I* sound.

Then have her cut out her pattern and softly say, "Insect," as she applies each of several stickers to it. Display the resulting projects on a bulletin board for an instant reminder of the letter *I*. *Insect* begins with /i/. How interesting!

Inchworm Puppets

Inching along, these inchworms might be just what your children need to lead them on a hunt for words beginning with the short *I* sound. Make a tagboard cutout of the inchworm pattern (page 57) for each child. Have him personalize his inchworm by coloring or painting it as desired and adding facial features with a fine-tip marker. When the decorating is complete, help him cut out his pattern and tape a large craft stick to the back of it to make a puppet. Then challenge students to inch their way around the classroom with their inchworms to look for objects whose names begin with short *I*. Let the hunt begin!

Iguana Begins Like *Igloo*

This fast-paced word game will inspire your little ones to listen for and name short *I* words. Say the word *igloo* and have students repeat it back to you. Emphasize the beginning short *I* sound for students to hear. Name other words that begin like *igloo.* For each short *I* word you say, ask each student to touch her index finger to her nose and then remove it as she repeats the word. After several rounds with words such as *iguana, inch, is, it, in,* and *invent,* name a few words that don't begin with *I,* such as *dog* or *cat,* to keep your little ones' listening skills sharp. Later, give students a turn at naming short *I* words, or change the game to focus on the long *I* sound, as in *ice.*

Picture This!

Pictures are the key to this fun phonemic activity. Make five picture cards that show objects whose names begin with short *I*. Also make five picture cards that show objects whose names begin with one letter other than *I*. Display the cards faceup and in random order at a center. Put a large colorful paper clip on one card from each set. Have each of two students select one of the marked cards. Have each child, in turn, name the picture on his marked card and then select another card with the same beginning sound. If the beginning sounds match, the child keeps the unmarked card. If the sounds do not match, he puts the card back. In either case, his turn ends. The possibilities for beginning-letter practice go on and on as new sets of beginning sounds are introduced.

Letter *I* Search

Students will enjoy spying the letter *I* in this print-rich activity. In large print on a chart or chalkboard, write a list of words that begin with short *I*. Tell students they are going to be investigators looking for the letter *I*. Give a magnifying lens to one child and ask her to find a word that begins with the letter *I*. Lead the class in celebrating her find and then read the word aloud for your students. Repeat the activity with different students. Then emphasize how the beginning sounds are alike. Repeat as interest allows. Leave the magnifying lens near the word list for impromptu searches by your little investigators.

insect

in

ill

if

I Riddles

Share these riddles with your students and watch vocabulary increase along with letter-sound correspondence skills. Write the riddle answers shown below in random order on a chart and highlight the beginning *I* in each word. Discuss each of the words and ask students to offer their ideas about each word's meaning. Next, point out the highlighted letter and ask students what the words have in common. Finally, read the provided clues aloud and have volunteers name the word that matches each clue. If students master short *I* vocabulary, try the game with some long *I* words.

Riddle	Answer
This is another word for *baby.*	infant
These are used to play music.	instruments
This is another word for *bug.*	insect
This is the opposite of *out.*	in
This is what makes you scratch your skin.	itch
This is a house made of ice.	igloo

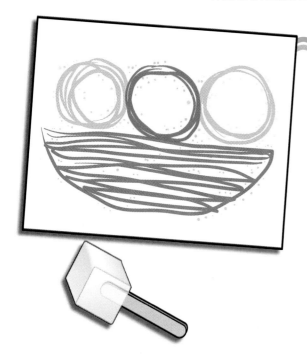

Ice Painting

When your little ones are ready to focus on the long sound of *I,* use these ice cube painters to introduce the sound. In advance, fill ice cube trays with water, cover them with plastic wrap, and insert a craft stick through the wrap into each compartment. Freeze the trays. Also prepare shakers that contain different colors of dry tempera paint. To make a painting, each child shakes dry paint onto a sheet of fingerpaint paper and then draws on the paper with an ice cube painter. Have students repeat the sound of long *I* (as in *ice*) or name other words that begin like *ice* as they paint. By the time your Picassos are done painting, they'll have a new vocabulary of long *I* words.

Ice-Cream Counting

Of all the long *I* words in the world, *ice cream* just may be the yummiest! In advance, cut five felt ice-cream cones and number them from 1 to 5. Also cut out 15 felt ice-cream scoops. Arrange the cones in order on a flannelboard and place the scoops nearby. To begin, write the word *ice cream* on a chart and talk about its beginning letter and its sound. Then have students take turns adding scoops to each cone to match the number on it. Now that's a double scoop of learning—identifying the initial sound of long *I* and counting to five!

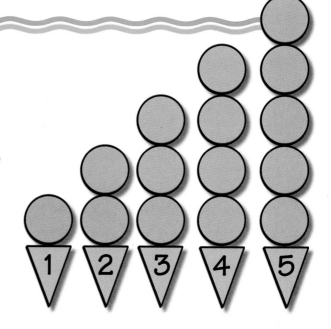

Incredible *I* Moves

- Scoot like an inchworm.
- Crawl or fly like an insect.
- Crawl like an infant.
- Pretend to play an instrument.

I Snacks

- ice cream
- iced tea
- icing on cake or graham crackers

I Ice-Cream Shop

Turn your dramatic-play area into an ice-cream shop by adding bowls, spoons, clean containers from ice cream or sprinkles, etc. Also set out materials for students to use to create signs, placemats, and menus.

The Ice-Cream Shop Song
(sung to the tune of "Did You Ever See a Lassie?")

Come with me to the ice-cream shop,
   ice-cream shop, ice-cream shop.
Come with me to the ice-cream shop for
   an icy treat.
They have lots of flavors
And cones topped with sprinkles!
Come with me to the ice-cream shop for
   an icy treat!

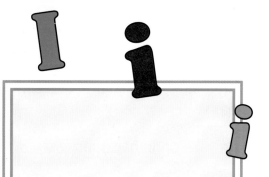

I Parade

Plan an *I* parade with your little ones! Pick and choose from the following costume and prop ideas. Then teach the provided song and let the marching begin!

Costumes

- inchworm (pillowcase with arm and head openings)

- insect wings and antennae headbands

- ice skater

- ice-cream parlor worker

Props

- ice-cream scoop

- instruments

- ice cube trays

- inchworm puppets (see page 52)

The *I* Parade Song
(sung to the tune of "When Johnny Comes Marching Home")

The *I*s are marching into town. Hooray! Hooray!
The *I*s are marching in a great big *I* parade.
Some have ice skates and ice-cream scoops.
Some have puppets with inchworms too.
Oh, we're so glad the *I*s could come today.

The *I*s are marching into town. Hooray! Hooray!
They're all so interesting; we hope they stay.
Some have instruments that play in tune.
Some have insects that fly round the room.
Oh, we're so glad the *I*s could come today.

I Pattern

Use with "*I* Is for *Insect*" on page 52.

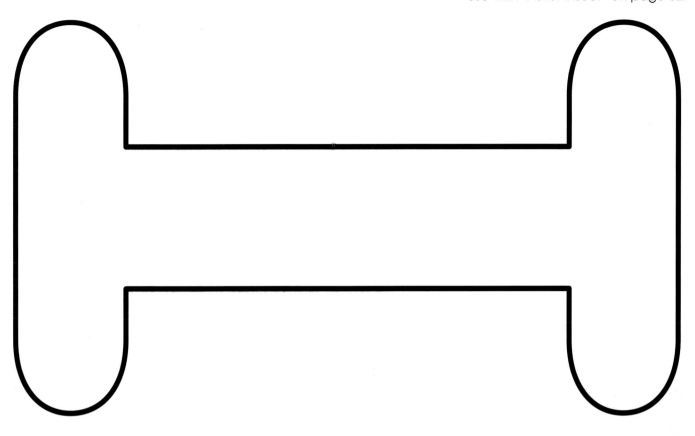

Inchworm Pattern

Use with "Inchworm Puppets" on page 52.

The Letter J

Jeweled Js

Add sparkle to your letter *J* study with this jewel of an activity! In advance, cut a supply of small jewel shapes from shiny foil wrapping paper and make a construction paper copy of the *J* pattern on page 63 for each child. Write the word *jewel* on the board and encourage students to say the beginning letter and sound they hear in this word. Then give each child a *J* pattern and have her glue jewel shapes onto it as desired.

Jumping Jack Puppets

This puppet will add bounce to your letter *J* activities! Make a construction paper copy of the puppet pattern on page 63 and cut five 1" x 9" strips of paper for each child. At circle time, ask a few youngsters at a time to stand and do several jumping jacks. Ask your group to say the sound they hear at the beginning of *jump* and *jack.* Then give each child a copy of the pattern to color and cut out. Next, give him four of the strips and show him how to accordion-fold them to make arms and legs for the puppet. Help him glue the arms and legs onto his puppet before setting it aside. Then, when the glue is dry, help him fold the last strip in half and tape it onto the back of the puppet to use as a handle.

Jet Skywriting

Swoop into letter writing with this fun fingerpaint activity! Ask students to watch as you write a large *J* on the board. Then have each child write a *J* in the air as he says the /j/ sound. Next, give each child a large sheet of paper and place a dollop of blue or black fingerpaint in the center of it. Have each child spread the paint across the paper to make a daytime or nighttime sky. Then have him pretend one of his fingers is a jet swooping down onto the paper to write an uppercase and a lowercase *J.*

Jack-in-the-Box

Jump into phonemic-awareness skills! Read the rhyme below to your group, encouraging them to listen for the /j/ sound at the beginning of words. Then ask students to stand up. Reread the rhyme and have students jump each time they hear a word that begins with the /j/ sound.

Jack-in-the-Box jumped out of his box
To see what he could see.
He saw some juicy jelly beans
And jam for biscuits and tea.

He saw some supersonic jets.
He saw some jazzy jeeps.
He saw a jolly jester
With jingle bells on his feet.

He saw a jet-black jaguar
At the Jackson zoo.
He saw jiggly jellyfish
And jumping kangaroos.

J Word Search

Focus on letter- and word-recognition skills with this easy-to-implement idea. Choose for your literacy center several books which feature words that begin with *J,* such as *Jump, Frog, Jump; Jack and the Beanstalk*; or a nursery rhyme collection. Choose one of the selections to read aloud to youngsters. Encourage them to listen for words that begin with the /j/ sound. Then review each page with students and place a sticky note underneath each word that begins with *J.* Later, when youngsters visit the book center, encourage them to search for words that begin with *J* and mark each one with a sticky note.

Jump up.
Jump down.

Jump in.
Jump out.

Jet Landing

Target letter *J* with this small-group activity that has youngsters flying through letter identification practice. To prepare, gather a supply of alphabet letter cutouts with a few extra *J* cutouts (see the pattern on page 63). Spread the letters on the floor in an open area, and make a paper jet. Invite a student to toss the jet toward the letters, aiming for a *J*. Ask the child to name the letter nearest where the jet landed. If it landed on a *J,* have her name it and then pick it up. Continue in this manner until all the *J*s are collected.

Giant Jelly Bean Jar

Join all your little sweeties together for this sorting activity. In advance, cut a large jelly bean from colorful construction paper for each child. During circle time, ask students to pretend they are sitting in a giant jelly bean jar. Give each child a jelly bean cutout and discuss the beginning /j/ sound of *jelly* and *jar.* Encourage one child at a time to say a sentence including the color of his jelly bean, such as "I'm a red jelly bean!" Then help youngsters move around to sort into jelly bean color groups inside the giant jar. Have each color group count its jelly beans. Then lead students in comparing the total number of jelly beans among the groups.

Joker Jostle

This hide-and-seek activity will bring out the joker every time! To prepare, gather two decks of playing cards. Remove the joker cards from both decks and hide all but one of them in different locations while students are out of the room. During circle time, show youngsters the remaining joker card and discuss the beginning /j/ sound. Ask students to name other words that begin with the /j/ sound and record their answers on a chart. Then invite a small group of students to search the room for the joker cards. When all the cards are found, have students return to the circle and each name a word that begins with the /j/ sound. Repeat the activity at a later time until each child has had a turn finding a joker.

Jolly J Moves

- Do jumping jacks.
- Fly like a jet.
- Jog in place.
- Dance a jig.
- Jump like a frog.
- Jump over a candle like Jack Be Nimble.

J Snacks

- jam or jelly on bread
- juice
- frozen juice pops
- Jell-O Jigglers gelatin snacks

J Café

Stock your dramatic-play area with items to create a *J* café. Include plastic jars, plastic juice pitchers, plastic jugs, and play foods from the list above. Also set out materials for your students to use to create signs, placemats, and menus.

The *J* Café Song
(sung to the tune of "Are You Sleeping?")

J cafe, *J* café—
Special treats, good to eat.
Jars and jars of jelly beans,
Juice and jam tarts—
Special treats—good to eat.

J Parade

Plan a *J* parade with youngsters! Pick and choose from the following costume and prop ideas. Then teach the provided song and let the marching begin!

Costumes

- jester hats
- jewelry
- jackets
- jeans
- jumpers
- jogging suits
- jeweled crowns
  (Glue shiny paper jewel shapes onto a headband crown.)

Props

- jack-in-the-boxes
- toy jeeps
- toy jets
- jump ropes
- plastic jack-o'-lanterns
- plastic juice pitchers
- plastic jars

The *J* Parade Song
*(sung to the tune of
"When Johnny Comes Marching Home")*

The *J*s are marching into town. Hooray! Hooray!
The *J*s are marching in a great big *J* parade.
Some jump rope and some drive jeeps.
Some have jingle bells on their feet.
Oh, we're so glad the *J*s could come today.

The *J*s are marching into town. Hooray! Hooray!
Some are tossing jelly beans as they come our way.
Some are juggling, see them now.
Some juggle jewels, I don't know how.
Oh, we're so glad the *J*s could come today.

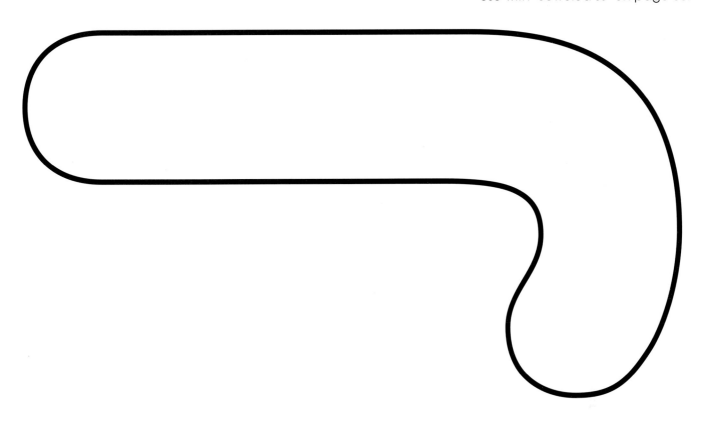

Puppet Pattern
Use with "Jumping Jack Puppets" on page 58.

The Letter K

K Is for *Kiss*

No lipstick is necessary to make these well-kissed *K*s! Cut lip-shapes from several kitchen sponges and place them at your art center with shallow containers of red paint (or use lip-shaped rubber stamps and ink pads). Enlarge the *K* pattern on page 69. Then make a class supply on white construction paper. To begin, invite a small group of students to your art table and give each child a pattern. Have each youngster make kiss prints on and around the *K* by dipping a prepared sponge into the paint and then repeatedly pressing it on his paper. Allow time for the paint to dry. Then have students take their projects home to share with their families!

Kite Puppets

Letter-writing skills soar with this colorful kite activity! Give each child a white construction paper copy of the kite pattern (page 69). Have him use a marker to draw a face on the kite and then use colorful crayons to draw capital *K*s around the face. Hole-punch the bottom of the kite. Then have each child choose several lengths of colorful curling ribbon. Thread the ribbon through the hole to resemble a tail. Then use tape to secure the ribbon ends to the back of the kite. Finally, encourage each youngster to tape a jumbo craft stick to the back of the kite to make a stick puppet.

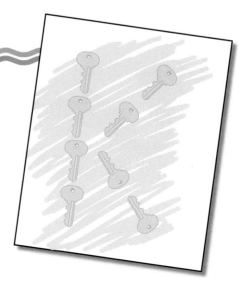

The Key to K

Unlock the door to literacy skills with this reminder of the letter *K* and its sound! Gather a supply of old keys and tape them to a tabletop in the shape of the letter *K*. Invite children to the table and have them place a sheet of copy paper over the *K* and then rub the side of a peeled crayon over the paper. When the *K* reveals itself, encourage each child to tell you the letter's sound!

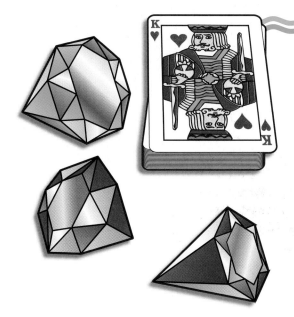

Where Are the Kings?

Youngsters get royal treatment when they search for kings with this card activity! Invite a small group of students to the table. Place a stack of playing cards in the center of the table and have youngsters take turns drawing a card. The first child to draw a king gets to hold the king's treasure (colorful jumbo decorator stones or chunky costume jewelry). Point out the *K* on the card and have youngsters say its sound. Then encourage students to continue drawing cards. As each king is drawn, have the king's treasure change hands to the child that drew the card. At the end of the game, allow each child the opportunity to inspect the treasure.

Four Little Kittens

These cute little kittens didn't lose any mittens—but they did find a whole bunch of items that begin with *K!* Write the rhyme provided on chart paper and post it in your circle-time area. Lead students in reciting the rhyme. Then invite youngsters to the chart paper to circle the *K*s!

Four little kittens went for a walk.
One found a ketchup bottle down the block.
Three little kittens walked on and on.
One found a key on the lawn.
Two little kittens climbed up high.
One found a kite up in the sky.
One little kitten went to the zoo.
She played with her friend Katie Kangaroo.

K Display

With this flannelboard game, youngsters review words that begin with the /k/ sound and improve their memories to boot! Gather or make picture cards that show items with names that begin with the /k/ sound, such as a kite, a king, a kangaroo, and a key. Prepare the cards for flannelboard use and then place them on your flannelboard. Have students say the name of each picture, prompting them to listen carefully for the /k/ sound. Then have students close their eyes. While their eyes are closed, remove a picture. Next, invite them to open their eyes and tell you which picture is missing. Now where is that kangaroo?

Fly a Kite

You're sure to grab youngsters' attention when you bring a real kite to school for your study of letter *K!* Before presenting the kite, have youngsters review what a *K* looks like and the sound it makes. Then reveal the kite with much fanfare. Encourage students to touch the kite and say its name as they carefully listen for the /k/ sound. If possible, take the kite outside for youngsters to experience the thrill of kite flying!

So Many Kings

A king need friends too! Youngsters identify the initial sound in a word to join a company of kings! In advance, make a simple crown for each child out of bulletin board border as shown. Don't forget to make one for yourself also! Gather or make a supply of picture cards, making sure that many of the pictures have names that begin with the /k/ sound. To begin, place a crown on your head and explain that kings get lonely and need other kings to keep them company. Show each child a picture card and prompt her to identify whether the word begins with the /k/ sound. Then place a crown on her head and invite her to join your group of kings. When each child has a crown, read or chant traditional king rhymes, such as "Old King Cole" or "Sing a Song of Sixpence." Everyone will love being king for a day!

A Classic K Story

What rhyme is the perfect accompaniment to a unit on the letter *K?* "The Three Little Kittens," of course! Obtain a copy of this nursery rhyme in book form. Introduce youngsters to the book and have them study the cover carefully. Invite students to point out the letter *K* in the title, and have students say the word *kittens* as they listen carefully for the /k/ sound. Then, as you read through the story, allow students to supply the word *kittens* each time it occurs!

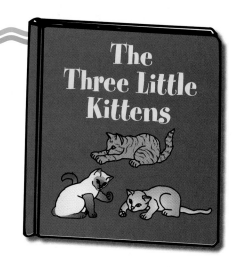

The Three Little Kittens

Kicky *K* Moves

- Kick pretend footballs.
- Pounce like a kitten.
- Jump like a kangaroo.
- Pretend to paddle a kayak.
- Move like King Kong.

K Snacks

- kiwi fruit slices
- sunflower seed kernels
- hot dogs sliced in thin strips and served with ketchup
- kabobs (Slide fruit pieces or cheese and meat slices on a straw.)

K Café

Stock your dramatic-play area with items to create a *K* café. Include kettles, kitchen utensils, empty ketchup bottles, cans of kidney beans, and empty Kool-Aid boxes. Also set out materials for your children to use to create signs, placemats, and menus.

The *K* Café Song
(sung to the tune of "Jingle Bells")

K café, *K* café
Full of special treats.
Let's go there and have lunch.
It's just down the street!

Kidney beans, kiwi fruit—
Oh, what should I eat?
Kool-Aid drinks and ketchup too—
This menu can't be beat!

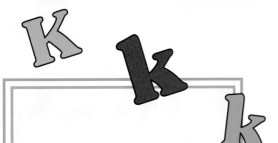

K Parade

Plan a *K* parade with your youngsters! Pick and choose from the following costume and prop ideas. Then teach the provided song and let the marching begin!

Costumes

- kitten ear headbands

- karate uniforms

- king crowns and robes (A large colorful beach towel can be made into a robe by simply draping it over a child's shoulders.)

Props

- stuffed kittens, koala bears, and kangaroos

- empty ketchup bottles

- keys

- kites

The *K* Parade Song
(sung to the tune of "When Johnny Comes Marching Home")

The *K*s are marching into town. Hooray! Hooray!
The *K*s are marching in a great big *K* parade.
Some have kites that fly way up high.
Some jingle keys as they walk by.
Oh, we're so glad the *K*s could come today.

The *K*s are marching into town. Hooray! Hooray!
Some are blowing kisses as they come our way.
Some are kings that have lovely crowns.
Some hold kittens and walk around.
Oh, we're so glad the *K*s could come today.

K Pattern

Use with *"K* Is for *Kiss"* on page 64.

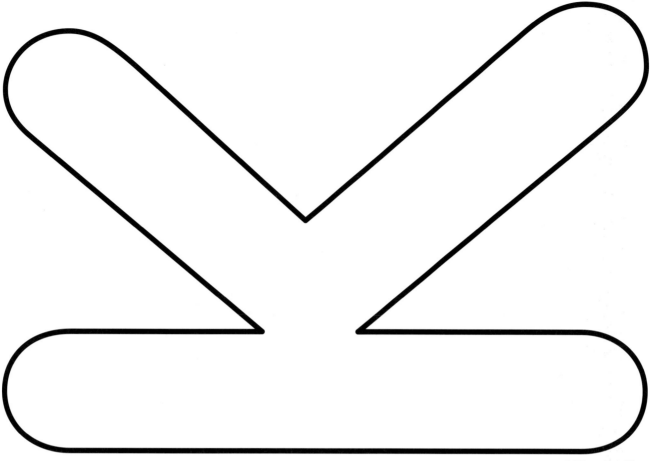

Kite Pattern

Use with "Kite Puppets" on page 64.

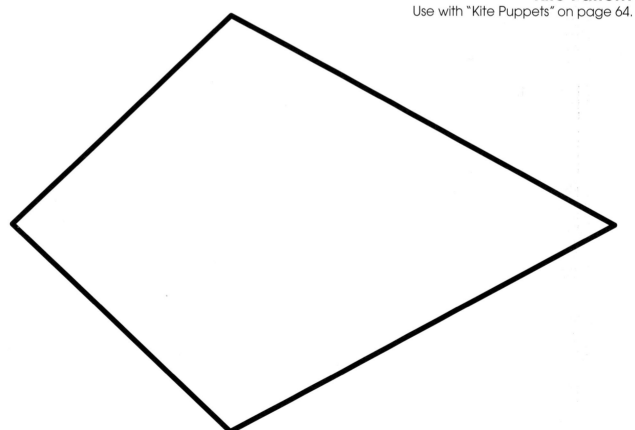

The Letter L

Ladybug, Ladybug

Your little ones will go buggy over this fine-motor activity, which helps develop letter-sound awareness. Give each child a white construction paper copy of the *L* pattern (page 75), and have him cut it out. Provide an ink pad with washable red ink and a small ladybug rubber stamp. Encourage each child to stamp ladybugs on his cutout. As he does this, encourage him to softly say other words that begin like *ladybug. Leap, love, like, luck,* and lots and lots of *ladybugs!*

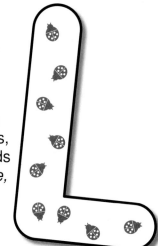

Lamb Puppets

These little lamb puppets are just right to incorporate into your letter *L* activities. Use the lamb pattern (page 75) as a tracer to make a class supply of tagboard lambs. Provide each child with a lamb cutout and access to cotton balls, markers, an old paintbrush, and a shallow container of glue. Have her lightly paint the body of the lamb cutout with glue and then gently pull apart a cotton ball and press it into the glue. Encourage her to continue placing cotton balls on the glue until the area is covered. When the glue is dry, have the child use markers to draw facial features. On the back of each project, write "[Child's name]'s Little Lamb" and tape a craft stick in place to make a puppet. To conclude, have each child point to the letter *L* in *lamb,* say the word, and listen for the /l/ sound.

Lacing *L*s

Look! It's time to build letter-formation awareness while sharpening fine-motor skills. Using a copy of the *L* pattern on page 75 as a tracer, make a class supply of poster board *L* shapes. Hole-punch around the edges and tie a length of yarn to one hole. Wrap the other end of the yarn length with tape to prevent fraying. Then give each child a prepared lacing *L,* and encourage her to lace the yarn through each hole to get a feel for the letter's shape.

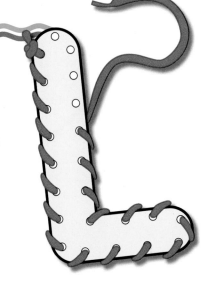

Letters to Deliver!

Here's a first-class idea for delivering letter-recognition skills! Gather two different colors of envelopes. Program each envelope of one color with an uppercase *L* and each of the other envelopes with a lowercase *L*. (If desired, glue a canceled stamp to each envelope.) Store the letters in a tote bag. Also, prepare color-coordinated mailboxes by covering two shoeboxes (and lids) with paper to match each envelope color and cutting an envelope-size slit in the top of each box. Above the slit, write the matching letter *L*. Place the mailboxes and the tote bag at a center. Invite each child, in turn, to sort the mail by delivering it to the appropriate mailbox.

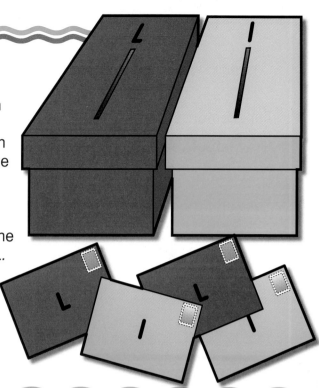

Sounds Like a Great Story!

Focus on letter-sound awareness during storytime! Choose a familiar tale to read to your youngsters, making sure that the title contains at least one word that begins with *L*. (Examples include *Little Red Riding Hood, The Three Little Pigs,* or a nursery rhyme such as "Little Boy Blue.") Write the title on the board and read it aloud. Ask students to name the word that begins with the /l/ sound. Then circle the letter. Invite students to make a special signal, such as holding up a thumb and forefinger to make an *L*, whenever they hear the /l/ sound. Then read the story, pausing to check for the special signal as appropriate. Later, expand this activity to include stories about lambs, ladybugs, and leaves. Sounds great!

L Opposites

Explore opposites with this word game that features lots of *L* words! Gather students and explain that you're going to say a word and you would like a volunteer to name its opposite. Further explain that each opposite begins with the /l/ sound. Then announce a word from the list and ask a volunteer to name its opposite. Continue in this same manner with the remaining words on the list. Conclude the activity by congratulating your little learners on a job well done!

short (long)

early (late)

dark (light)

big (little)

small (large)

tight (loose)

I like lemons. I like limes.

How about you? Do you like them too?

L foods are fun. Let's eat every one.

Some for me. Some for you.

Love Those *L* Foods!

Here's a tasteful little ditty that's sure to whet your youngsters' appetites for the letter *L!* To prepare, copy the song shown onto a chart (without circling the *L*s). Then teach children the words and tune. After singing the song several times, ask each of several volunteers to take a turn circling an *L* in the text. Next, enlist students' help in creating additional verses featuring *L* foods such as lasagna, lettuce, lentils, lobster, lollipops, and linguine. Write the verses on the chart and invite volunteers to circle the *L*s.

Ladybugs on Leaves

Reinforce awareness of the /l/ sound during counting practice by using ladybugs and leaves! To prepare, cut five large leaves from green construction paper. Program each leaf with a different number from 1 to 5. Stamp a ladybug onto each of 15 construction paper circles and color them as desired. Laminate all the pieces for durability and place them at a center. A child reads the number on a leaf and then counts out the matching number of ladybugs. For more language practice, have him softly count aloud as he creates each ladybug set. One, two, three, four, five ladybugs on this leaf!

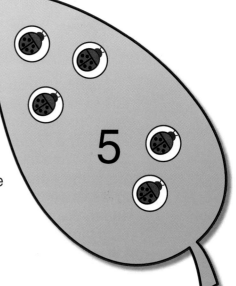

I sorted the long leaves.

Leaf Sort

Lots of lovely leaves bring letter awareness to sorting practice! In advance, collect three to four silk leaves in each of several types. Mix up the leaves and place them in a basket. Invite a child to take a turn sorting the leaves by type. Then have him describe the leaves and his sorting rule. Help him write a sentence about his sorting experience, making sure to point out all the examples of the letter *L.* Then have him highlight each *L,* paying special attention to the *L* in *leaves.*

Lovely *L* Moves

- Leap like a lizard.
- Roar like a lion.
- Frolic like a lamb.
- Roll like a log.
- Dance like a leprechaun.
- Pretend to climb a ladder.

L Snacks

- lemonade
- cooked lentils
- linguine
- lasagna
- lettuce
- cups of water with lemon or lime slices
- lemon meringue pie
- safety lollipops

Lemonade Stand

Stock your dramatic-play area with items to create a lemonade stand! Provide three-ounce paper cups and the listed ingredients to make fresh lemonade (see the recipe below). Each day, invite a small group of students to prepare a batch of lemonade and then serve it to classmates. For more fun, have the stand workers sing "Lemonade Stand Song" below. How refreshing!

Lemonade Stand Song
(sung to the tune of "Are You Sleeping?")

Lemonade, lemonade
Hits the spot when it's hot.
We made it nice and sweet.
Come have a fresh-made treat—
Lemonade, lemonade.

Old-Fashioned Lemonade

3 c. cold water
juice of four lemons (about 1 c.)
½ c. sugar

Put the ingredients into a plastic pitcher. Stir briskly with a wooden spoon until the sugar dissolves (about 2 minutes). Serve cold.

L Parade

Plan an *L* parade with your little ones! Pick and choose from the following costume and prop ideas. Then teach the provided song and let the marching begin!

Costumes

- lion masks
- lamb masks
- leotards
- ladybug hats
- leprechaun hats
- lace shawls

Props

- lunchboxes
- toy ladders
- large cardboard letters
- lids
- lanterns
- large cardboard lollipops
- silk leaves
- lemon and lime shakers (Collect empty, clean, plastic lemon- or lime-shaped juice containers. Remove the lids and plugs. Pour a spoonful of rice into the container; then replace the plug and hot-glue the lid in place.)

The *L* Parade Song
(sung to the tune of "When Johnny Comes Marching Home")

The *L*s are marching into town. Hooray! Hooray!
The *L*s are marching in a great big *L* parade.
Some have lanterns; some have lambs.
Some carry lace right in their hands.
Oh, we're so glad the *L*s could come today!

The *L*s are marching into town. Hooray! Hooray!
Some throw leaves as they come our way today.
Some have lemons or lollipops.
Some like to leap around a lot.
Oh, we're so glad the *L*s could come today!

L Pattern
Use with "Ladybug, Ladybug" and "Lacing *Ls*" on page 70.

Lamb Pattern
Use with "Lamb Puppets" on page 70.

The Letter M

Marshmallow Print Ms

This art activity is a sweet way to remind youngsters of the /m/ sound. Make an enlarged copy of the *M* pattern on page 81 on dark construction paper for each child and cut it out. Distribute the cutouts; then supply each child with a large marshmallow and access to a pan containing a thin layer of white paint. Before beginning, talk about the beginning letter and sound in *marshmallow*. Have the child dip one end of his marshmallow in the paint and then press it on his paper as he says the /m/ sound. Have him continue in this same manner to make several prints on his paper. When the paper is dry, have each child use a marker to write an uppercase *M* on a few of the marshmallow prints. Mmm, marshmallows!

Sewing Mittens

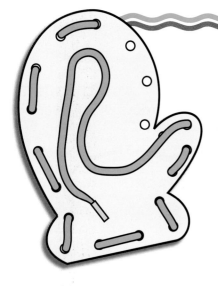

Letter recognition was never "sew" fun for students! Copy and cut out a mitten pattern (page 81) for each child. Punch evenly spaced holes around the perimeter of each mitten. Thread one end of a yarn length through a hole; then tie it in place. Wrap a piece of tape around the other end of the yarn to make lacing easier. Write the word *mitten* on the board. Help children name the beginning letter and listen for its sound as everyone says, "Mitten." Then give a prepared mitten to each child, and have him lace the yarn through the holes. When the lacing is complete, help him tie the yarn in place. Finally, have each child use a marker to program one side of the cutout with an uppercase and a lowercase *M* before decorating the other side as desired.

Mosaic Masterpieces

These colorful, mosaic creations are perfect for reinforcing the /m/ sound. In advance, cut various colors of construction paper into irregular-shaped pieces. Write the word *mosaic* on the board and explain to students that a mosaic is a picture made up of small colored pieces. If possible, show students some samples. Point out the beginning sound in *mosaic* and have students identify the initial consonant. Then give each child a sheet of white paper and a handful of the construction paper pieces. Each child sorts the pieces by colors, arranges them on a sheet of white paper to create a desired picture, and then glues them in place. Marvelous!

Sorting Mail

This learning center is a first-class way to spark interest in letter recognition. To prepare, label ten envelopes with words that begin with *M* and ten envelopes with words that begin with other letters. If desired, also glue a clip art picture of each word to the envelope. Store the envelopes in a tote bag and place the bag and a mailbox in a center. To use the center, a student pretends to be a mail carrier and sorts the envelopes into two groups. The envelopes labeled with *M* words go in the mailbox and the remaining envelopes go in a return-to-sender pile. Now that's a special delivery!

The Kittens' Mittens

Give little ones a chance to practice visual-discrimination skills with this game. In advance, gather enough pairs of mittens for each child to have one from a pair. (Each pair needs to look different.) To begin, give each child a mitten and have him slide it on his hand. Next, read aloud the nursery rhyme "The Three Little Kittens" and challenge students to raise their mitten-covered hands each time they hear the word *mitten*. Then, for added fun, challenge each youngster to find the student holding the mate to his mitten. No more lost mittens!

Mad Words

Introduce the *-ad* word family with this activity. To begin, write the word *mad* on a sheet of paper and talk about its meaning. Point to the beginning letter and its sound; then point out the *-ad* ending. Ask students to think of other words that end in this same manner. List students' responses on a chart. If desired, add a title, as shown, and post the chart in the classroom.

Mad About -ad Words

mad	dad
bad	pad
sad	tad
had	
lad	

Many Moons

Sorting skills take shape with this medley of moon phases. Tape a length of black paper to a table. Then cut 12 circles from white poster board. Cut four circles in half to make eight half moons. Trim two crescent shapes from each of four more circles to make eight crescent moons. Securely tape a progression of moon phases to the black paper as shown. Then stack the remaining three full moons, six half moons, and six crescent moons at the center. To begin, write the word *moon* on the board and talk about its beginning sound. Then show youngsters reference book pictures of different phases of the moon as you explain to them that the moon appears to change its shape in the sky. Have youngsters sort the cutouts atop the matching moon phases.

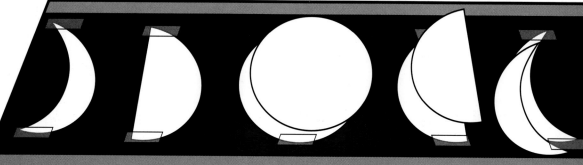

Monkeying Around With Estimation

Swing into estimation with this marvelous math activity! To prepare, fill a clear, empty lidded container with plastic monkeys. Present the jar to the class with great fanfare. Then write the word *monkey* on the board and point out the beginning letter. Have youngsters say the sound at the beginning of the word. Next, challenge each child to estimate the number of monkeys in the jar. List the responses on a chart and then discuss which estimates are the highest and lowest. Together, count the monkeys aloud. Then challenge students to determine whose guess was closest.

Mighty Magnets

Attract plenty of interest in magnets with this this *M*-related center! In advance, gather some magnets and a collection of magnetic and nonmagnetic items, and store them in a container. To begin, show students the magnets and write the word *magnet* on the board. Have students name the beginning letter and listen for its sound as everyone says, "Magnet." Then place the magnets and the container at a center. As students visit the center, encourage them to use the magnets to help them determine which items from the container are magnetic.

Marvelous *M* Moves

- Pretend to mop a messy floor.
- Swing like a monkey.
- Scurry like a mouse.
- Stomp like a monster.
- Pretend to drive a fast motorcycle.

M Snacks

- meatballs
- milk
- muffins
- melons
- mini marshmallows

M Café

Stock your dramatic-play area with items to create an *M* café. Include empty food packages and play foods from the list above along with items such as muffin tins, oven mitts, and a toy microwave. Also set out materials for students to use to create signs, placemats, and menus.

The *M* Café Song
(sung to the tune of "Are You Sleeping?")

M café, *M* café—
Special treats, good to eat.
Milk, muffins, marshmallows,
Macaroni, meatballs—
Special treats. Mmm, let's eat!

M Parade

Plan an *M* parade with your youngsters! Pick and choose from the following costume and prop ideas. Then teach the provided song and let the marching begin!

Costumes

- mittens

- monster costumes

- mail carrier bags

- masks

- mouse ears
(Glue two four-inch gray construction paper circles to a gray paper strip. Then staple the strip to make a headband that fits the child's head.)

Props

- mops

- maps

- play money

- stuffed monkeys and/or mice

- milk cartons

- marionettes

- maracas

- plastic mirrors

- marigolds

The *M* Parade Song
(sung to the tune of "When Johnny Comes Marching Home")

The *M*s are marching into town. Hooray! Hooray!
The *M*s are marching in a great big *M* parade.
Some throw money all around.
Some shake maracas up and down.
Oh, we're so glad the *M*s could come today!

The *M*s are marching into town. Hooray! Hooray!
Some ride motorcycles as they come our way.
Some wear masks and big mouse ears.
Some carry marigolds and makeup mirrors.
Oh, we're so glad the *M*s could come today!

M **Pattern**
Use with "Marshmallow Print *M*s" on page 76.

Mitten Pattern
Use with "Sewing Mittens" on page 76.

The Letter N

Oodles of Noodles

Wide noodles, thin noodles, long noodles! There are so many different noodles little ones can glue to this *N* pattern, the "pasta-bilities" are endless! Enlarge the *N* pattern on page 87. Then make a tagboard copy for each child. Have him trace the *N* with his finger and say its name. Invite each child to color his *N*. Next, provide access to a variety of noodles. Encourage each child to say the word *noodles,* listening carefully for the /n/ sound. Then have him glue noodles to his *N* until a desired effect is achieved.

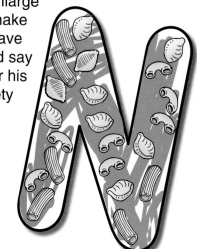

Nest Puppets

Be sure to include these unique nest puppets during your study of letter *N!* Make a brown construction paper copy of the nest pattern (page 87) for each child. Have each student cut out the pattern, and then helped her cut a slit where indicated. Have her glue pieces of yarn and raffia to the cutout to give it a nest-like appearance. After the glue dries, have each child slide her hand into the slit as shown so that her wiggling fingers resemble baby birds. Invite students to wear their puppets to circle time to assist them in practicing the letter *N* and its sound.

What's That Noise?

Woof! Dingdong! Vroom! Chirp! When youngsters identify a variety of noises, they are sure to sharpen their listening skills! In advance, record a variety of indoor and outdoor noises such as a car idling, a bird chirping, a vacuum cleaner running, and ice cubes clinking in a glass. Gather your youngsters and explain that you have recorded several noises. Have children repeat the word *noise* and listen carefully for the /n/ sound. Then play the first noise recorded and have students suggest what it might be. When the source of the noise is confirmed, move on to the next recording. This activity can't possibly get too noisy!

Nifty Nursery Rhymes

What better way to spotlight the letter *N* than by reading nursery rhymes! Each day throughout your study of the letter *N,* read a nursery rhyme aloud. (Consider focusing on rhymes that contain at least one main word that begins with *N,* such as "Jack Be Nimble.") Before reading the chosen rhyme for the day, write the phrase *nursery rhyme* on the board. Invite a youngster to circle the letter *N.* Then challenge students to listen for other words that begin with the /n/ sound as you read the rhyme.

Near and Far

The /n/ sound won't be far from your youngsters' minds with this playful position-word activity! Collect a variety of engaging objects, such as stuffed animals or large plastic dinosaurs. Make two tagboard signs labeled as shown. To begin, gather youngsters in your circle-time area. Choose two objects; place one near the students and the other a distance away from the students. Then hold up the signs and have them repeat the words *near* and *far.* Invite youngsters to identify the word that begins with the /n/ sound. Then encourage a student to place each sign next to the appropriate object. Repeat the game several times, placing different objects in new locations each time.

Covered With Newspaper

Extra! Extra! This cooperative activity is a memorable way to reinforce the shape of the letter *N!* Tape to a table a length of bulletin board paper labeled with a large letter *N.* Then provide access to glue and several sheets of newspaper. Invite one or more students to the table. Encourage each child to trace the letter with her hand as she says its name. Then have her say the word *newspaper,* listening carefully for the /n/ sound. Next, invite each youngster to tear pieces of newspaper and glue them to the *N.* When the *N* is completely covered with newspaper and each child has had an opportunity to visit the table, remove the paper and post it at student eye level. Encourage your little ones to visit the display and use their hands to trace the *N.*

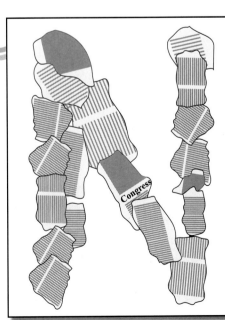

A Number of Nickels

Will this *N*-themed activity help youngsters with coin recognition? You can bank on it! Hot-glue a row of ten nickels to a ten-inch tagboard strip and write the word *nickels* under the row. After the glue cools, tape the strip to a table in a center. Provide access to a supply of copy paper and unwrapped crayons. Invite a child to the center. Have him say the word *nickels* and point to the letter *N*. Next, invite him to use the provided supplies to make a rubbing of the nickels. Finally, have him count the prints on his rubbing!

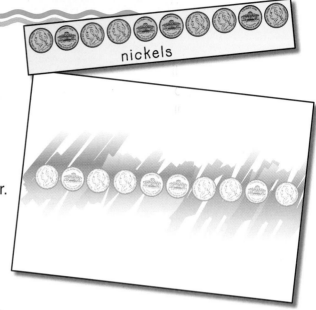

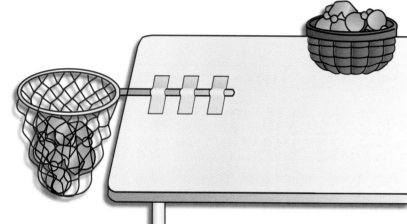

Netting Knee-Highs

Not only does this activity encourage youngsters to learn the /n/ sound, it also improves hand-eye coordination! Gather a small butterfly or fishing net and a supply of clean knee-highs. Securely tape the handle of the net to a tabletop so that the net hangs over the edge as shown. Several feet away from the net, place a tape line on the floor. Stuff a ball of cotton batting in the toe of each knee-high. Then knot the knee-highs so the batting stays in place. Place the knee-highs in a container next to the tape line. Gather youngsters and introduce them to the props. Encourage them to say the word *net* and listen carefully for the /n/ sound. Then invite a small group of students to the center. Each student, in turn, stands on the tape line and tries to toss a knee-high in the net. The students continue taking turns until all of the knee-highs have been tossed. What fun!

Napkins on the Table

Serve up a helping of letter-sound recognition with this activity, and students get a side dish of one-to-one correspondence too! Use a marker to write a large *N* on each of several colorful napkins to match the number of chairs at a table. Then invite a child to the table. Prompt him to identify the letter written on the napkins. Encourage him to fold the napkins in half and place one in front of each chair. (You may wish to have a session of folding practice before this center is open for business!) When students are comfortable with this duty, add plastic plates, cups, and utensils to the center for youngsters to practice setting the table.

Nimble N Moves

- Roll like a nut.
- Flop around like a cooked noodle.
- Do nine jumping jacks, toe touches, or other appropriate exercises.
- Pretend to read a newspaper.
- Wiggle your nose.
- Pretend to pound a nail with a hammer.

N Snacks

- nachos
- nectarines
- noodles
- Neapolitan ice cream
- chicken nuggets

N Café

Stock your dramatic-play area with items to create an *N* café. Include empty food packages and play foods from the list above. Also set out materials for students to use to create signs, placemats, and menus.

The *N* Café Song
(sung to the tune of "Jingle Bells")

N café, *N* café,
Full of special treats.
Let's go and have some lunch.
It's just down the street!

Nectarines, navy beans,
Nachos full of cheese!
Neapolitan ice cream—
I'll have two scoops, please!

N Parade

Plan an *N* parade with your youngsters! Pick and choose from the following costume and prop ideas. Then teach the provided song and let the marching begin!

Costumes

- neckties

- funny noses

- nurse uniforms, caps, and accessories such as play stethoscopes

- nursery rhyme characters

- nightgowns (worn over school clothes)

Props

- large tagboard numbers

- nets

- newspapers

- nursery rhyme books

- nests (found at craft stores)

The *N* Parade Song
(sung to the tune of "When Johnny Comes Marching Home")

The *N*s are marching into town. Hooray! Hooray!
The *N*s are marching in a great big *N* parade!
Some wear neckties and some nightgowns.
We all make noise as we march to town.
Oh, we're so glad the *N*s could come today.

The *N*s are marching into town. Hooray! Hooray!
Some are holding numbers as they march our way.
Some have newspapers; some have nets.
Some wear noses and carry nests.
Oh, we're so glad the *N*s could come today.

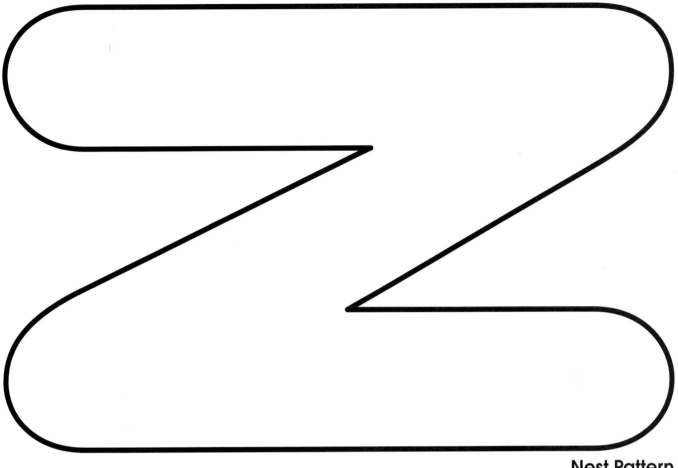

Nest Pattern
Use with "Nest Puppets" on page 82.

The Letter O

Only Os

Just look to your local office supply store—or your desk drawer—to find the perfect item for youngsters to use to decorate the letter *O!* In advance, gather a supply of white hole reinforcers. Enlarge the *O* pattern on page 93. Then make a colorful construction paper copy of the pattern for each child. Encourage each student to trace the *O* with her finger while she says its name. Then have her cut out the pattern, providing assistance if necessary. Next, invite each youngster to stick several little *O*s (hole reinforcers) to the cutout. Display the resulting projects on a bulletin board or classroom wall.

Octopus Puppet

Give students a leg up on the short *O* sound with this adorable octopus puppet! For each child, make two construction paper copies of the octopus pattern (page 93) and eight ½" x 7" construction paper strips. With the curved edge at the top, have each student draw a face on one of the patterns. Then encourage him to flip the pattern over and glue the strips (tentacles) to the bottom edge. After the glue dries, staple the second pattern to the back of the octopus (leaving the bottom open) to make a pocket. Then have each student curl the tentacles by briefly wrapping each one around a thick pencil or marker. Invite each youngster to slip his octopus on a hand. Then recite several familiar words. After each word beginning with the short *O* sound, have children wiggle the puppet's tentacles and say, "/o/, /o/, octopus!"

Orange Prints

This zestful printmaking activity is a fun way to focus on the letter *O*—with the added bonus of giving your art area a lovely citrus scent! In advance, obtain three oranges and slice each one in half. Cut two notches in each half, as shown, to make a handle. Dry the orange halves overnight. Then place them at your art table along with shallow trays of orange tempera paint. To begin, write the word *orange* on the board and have youngsters point out the letter *O* at the beginning of the word. Then have each youngster make orange prints on a sheet of 12" x 18" white construction paper until a desired effect is achieved. When the paint is dry, encourage her to use a marker to write the word *orange* at the bottom of her painting.

orange

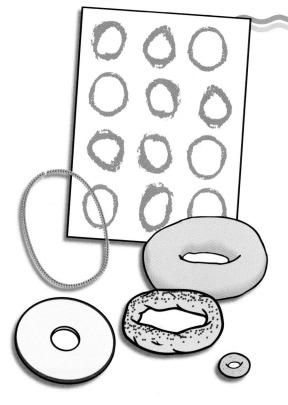

So Many *O*s

Youngsters can experience the shape of the letter *O* in so many ways! Choose one—or several—of the suggestions provided. For each activity, prompt each child to trace the *O* and then say the letter's name.

- Give each youngster a piece of refrigerated breadstick dough. Have him form the dough into an *O* and then sprinkle cinnamon and sugar on top. Bake the dough according to the package directions.
- Have youngsters manipulate chenille stems into *O*s.
- Have each child use an orange crayon to write *O*s on a sheet of paper.
- Core an apple and slice it into crosswise sections to resemble the letter *O*. Give each child several sections as a snack.
- Provide one of several *O*-shaped treats, such as Cheerios cereal, bagels, or plain doughnuts.

O Toss

The props used in this ring-toss game are certain to remind your children of the letter *O*! In advance, gather a supply of large plastic lids (such as those that come on gallon-size ice-cream containers) and several two-liter bottles. Cut a large hole in the center of each lid. Remove the labels from the bottles and fill the bottles with water. Then screw on each cap and tape it in place. Use a permanent marker to label each bottle with either the letter *O* or a distractor letter. Place the bottles on the floor in a traffic-free area of the room. A child stands in a designated location and tries to toss the *O*-shaped rings on the bottles. When he is out of rings, he examines the bottles to see if he has ringed any labeled with the letter *O*!

A Lot of *-ot*

Your little ones will flip over this fun class book that focuses on the *-ot* word family! In advance, make a blank flip book with several pages as shown. Label the visible portion of the back page with "ot," spotlighting the letter *O* in red. Then write the letter *L* on the front page to make the word *lot.* To begin, show youngsters the book and read the word *lot.* Then encourage them to identify the letter *O*. Prompt students to name other words that end with *-ot*. For each appropriate suggestion, help youngsters identify the beginning sound in the word as you write it on a page. When each page has a letter, encourage students to chime in as you read the completed book!

An Obstacle Course

Under, over, and around—youngsters use some of their best moves to go through this obstacle course and find the letter *O* at the end! Set up an obstacle course in your school gymnasium or on the playground. At the end of the course, display a large letter *O*. To begin, explain that an obstacle course is a series of objects that a person has to go around, through, over, or under. Have children repeat the word *obstacle* and listen carefully for the short *O* sound in the beginning of the word. Then prompt youngsters to go through the course and touch the letter *O* at the end to show they are finished!

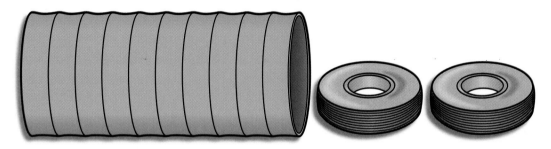

O Critters

Otters, ostriches, and octopi, oh my! With this activity, youngsters are sure to be fascinated with creatures whose names begin with *O*. Gather a collection of age-appropriate nonfiction books about the animals mentioned above. Write each animal's name on the board, and have students identify the *O* in each one. Then have the youngsters recite the names, listening carefully for the short *O* sound. Throughout your study of letter *O*, read aloud several of the chosen selections and pause occasionally to have volunteers locate *O*s in the text. Then place the books in your science center for independent reading!

Opposites

Little ones celebrate the letter *O* with this picture-perfect opposites display! Write the word *opposites* at the top of a sheet of chart paper. Have youngsters say the word and listen carefully for the short *O* sound at the beginning of the word. Prompt youngsters to share several opposites as you write each one down (see the suggestions given). Count up the words to ensure you have one per child. Then take a photograph of each youngster demonstrating one of the words. For example, a child could hold a pillow or a stuffed animal to show the word *soft*. (If you have an odd number of children, you or a classroom helper will also need to pose.) Display the pairs of photos on a bulletin board titled "Can You Name the Opposites?"

Suggested Opposites: over—under, hard—soft, on—off, right—left, new—old, open—close, sit—stand, smooth—bumpy, up—down, day—night, long—short, big—small

90

Original *O* Moves

- Move like an octopus.
- Run like an ostrich.
- Swim like an otter.
- Pretend to dive in the ocean.
- Roll like an orange.
- Shake like an oak tree.

O Snacks

- olives (pitted)
- omelettes
- orange juice
- oranges
- oatmeal cookies
- oatmeal

O Cafe

Stock your dramatic-play area with items to create an *O* café. Include empty food packages and play foods from the list above along with items such as an omelette pan and an orange juicer. Also set out materials for students to use to create signs, placemats, and menus.

The *O* Café Song
(sung to the tune of "Are You Sleeping?")

O café, *O* café,
Has some food we can eat:
Oranges round and sweet
And omelettes—what a treat!
Olives too, just for you!

O Parade

Plan an *O* parade with your youngsters! Pick and choose from the following costume and prop ideas. Then teach the provided song and let the marching begin!

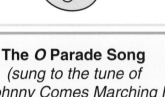

Costumes

- officer hats and badges
- overalls
- ocean-related gear (snorkels, goggles, floats, etc.)
- overcoats
- orange clothing

Props

- office supplies
- opera glasses
- oatmeal boxes
- oranges

The *O* Parade Song
(sung to the tune of "When Johnny Comes Marching Home")

The *O*s are marching into town. Hooray! Hooray!
The *O*s are marching in a great big *O* parade.
Some wear overalls and overcoats.
Some wear snorkels and carry bright floats.
Oh, we're so glad the *O*s could come today.

The *O*s are marching into town. Hooray! Hooray!
Some give out oatmeal cookies as they come our way.
There are octopi with tentacles long
That wiggle around as we sing this song.
Oh, we're so glad the *O*s could come today.

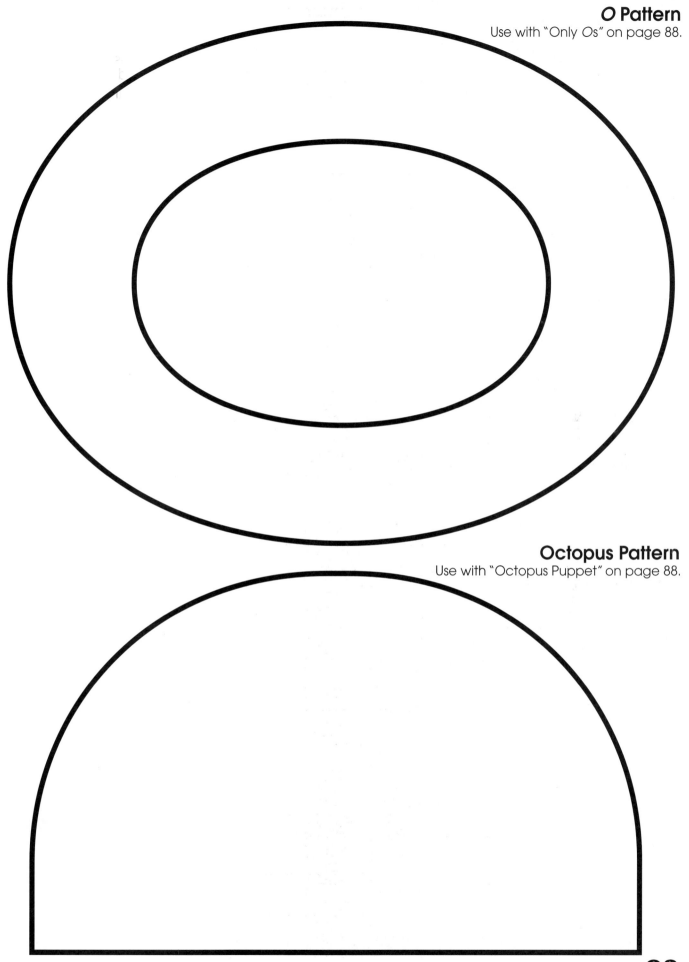

O **Pattern**
Use with "Only *Os*" on page 88.

Octopus Pattern
Use with "Octopus Puppet" on page 88.

The Letter P

Purple Ps

When little ones decorate *P*s with purple paraphernalia, "hue" won't believe the oohs and aahs that result! Gather a small group of children at your art center. Give each child a white construction paper copy of the *P* pattern (page 99) and provide access to a variety of purple craft items, such as chenille stems, pom-poms, tissue paper, paint, and glitter. Have each youngster say the word *purple* and listen carefully for the /p/ sound. Help each child cut out her pattern. Then invite her to glue a variety of items to her cutout until a desired effect is achieved. How pleasing!

Pig Puppets

Your youngsters will squeal in delight when they make these cute pig puppets! Gather a small group of students in your art area. Have each student cut out a pink construction paper copy of the pig pattern (page 99) and tape a jumbo craft stick to the back of the cutout to make a puppet. Set the puppet aside. Then invite each child to brush pink tempera paint on the outside of a small Dixie cup. Next, help him glue the Dixie cup to the front of the puppet to resemble a snout. When the puppet is dry, encourage each youngster to carefully use a permanent marker to draw eyes, a mouth, and nostrils on the pig. Have students bring their puppets to circle time to assist them in reviewing the letter *P* and its sound!

Pussywillow Plants

These pretty pussywillow paintings make a lovely classroom decoration and reinforce the /p/ sound! If possible, place a pussywillow clipping in a vase for children to touch and observe. If pussywillows do not grow in your area, show youngsters a picture of the plant. Then encourage them to say the word *pussywillow* and listen carefully for the /p/ sound. Next, give each child a 12" x 18" sheet of light blue construction paper. Have her use a brown marker to draw several branches on her paper. Then have each youngster dip a finger into a shallow tray of gray tempera paint and make prints along the branches to resemble pussywillows!

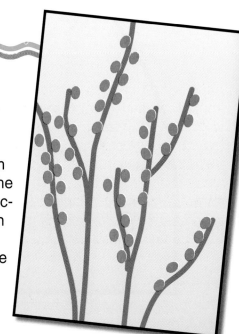

Plentiful *P* Folktales

Even if the sky really were falling, you wouldn't be able to drag youngsters away from this collection of engaging folktales! Obtain a version of each of the following folktales: *Henny Penny, The Princess and the Pea,* and *The Three Little Pigs.* Before reading each story, have students study the title and locate the *P*s. Then, as you read, stop occasionally to have youngsters repeat words that begin with the letter *P.*

P Riddles

Grab little ones' attention with a plethora of quick *P* riddles! Before presenting the following riddles to your students, explain that you'll share with them a hint for finding the answers—they all begin with the /p/ sound!

What is big, round, and grows in the garden? *(a pumpkin)*
What is pink, lives on a farm, and rolls in the mud? *(a pig)*
What is black and white and lives where it is cold? *(a penguin)*
What is eaten for breakfast with butter and syrup? *(a pancake)*
What do people wear on their legs? *(pants)*
What comes in a pod and is picked from a garden? *(a pea)*
What makes marks on paper and is often sharpened? *(a pencil)*

Plenty of Puppets

This puppet center is sure to be a popular destination for your students! To encourage pretend play, place at a center a variety of puppets along with several items that begin with the letter *P,* such as pillows, pinwheels, and plastic plants. Introduce the puppets and props to your youngsters, and have students isolate the sound at the beginning of each object's name. Then encourage students to use the puppets and props for pretend play. If desired, replace the props each day to ensure the center's continued popularity!

Planting a Garden

Cultivate your little gardeners' letter knowledge with plenty of plants! In advance, gather several plant seeds that begin with the letter *P,* such as petunias, peppers, peas, potatoes, and pumpkins. As youngsters help you plant the seeds, encourage them to repeat the names of the plants and listen carefully for the /p/ sound. Post each seed packet on the appropriate container for youngsters to use as a reference. Then have them water the plants and observe carefully when they begin to sprout. Place a supply of paper and crayons near your plant station for youngsters to use to copy the plants' names and illustrate their growth.

P Puzzles

These puzzles are a piece of cake to make, and your little ones will love the colorful results. Enlarge the *P* pattern on page 99. Make a copy of the pattern on pink construction paper and one on purple construction paper. Then laminate the papers for durability. Cut the patterns into large puzzle pieces, using the same puzzle cuts for each one. Then place the puzzles at a center. A child visits the center and puts the puzzles together, combining the pink and purple pieces. How pretty!

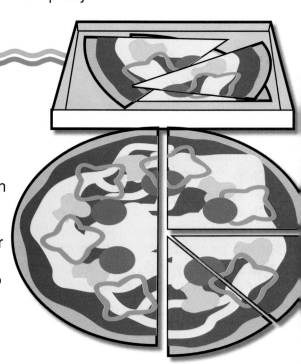

Pizza Pies

Big slice? Medium slice? Little slice? How about one of each? Children use spatial skills to put together pizzas with a variety of slices. In advance, make three 12-inch construction paper pizzas. Laminate the pizzas. Then cut one pizza in half, one into fourths, and one into eighths. Put the slices in a container. Place the container in a center along with a 12-inch circle of cardboard. Invite a child to the center. Have her say, "/p/, /p/, pizza," to help her hear the sound of the letter *P.* Then invite her to fit a variety of slices on the cardboard to make a whole pizza.

Powerful *P* Moves

- March in a parade.
- Pretend to flip pancakes.
- Pretend to pick peaches.
- Waddle like a penguin.
- Pretend to fly and squawk like a parrot.
- Pretend to play the piano.

P Snacks

- pickles
- peaches
- plums
- pears
- pretzels
- pineapple
- pie
- pepperoni pizza

P Café

Stock your dramatic-play area with items to create a *P* café. Include empty food packages and play foods from the list above along with items such as paper plates, pie tins, pots and pans, and pancake turners. Also set out materials for students to use to create signs, placemats, and menus.

The *P* Café Song
(sung to the tune of "Mary Had a Little Lamb")

Let's go to the *P* café,
P café, *P* café.
Let's go to the *P* café.
They have pizza pie.

They have peaches, pears, and plums,
Pears and plums, pears and plums.
They have peaches, pears, and plums
And pancakes stacked up high.

97

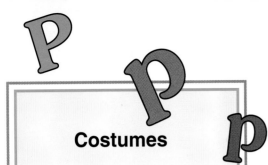

P Parade

Plan a *P* parade with your youngsters. Pick and choose from the following costume and prop ideas. Then teach the provided song and let the marching begin!

Costumes

- pilot hats
- police hats
- pants
- princess crowns
- plaid and polka-dot clothes

Props

- paper plates
- small pumpkins
- puppets
- pots and pans
- pillows
- pom-poms
  (Gather several tissue paper strips and fold the bundle in half. Wrap tape around the folded end to create a handle.)

The *P* Parade Song
(sung to the tune of "When Johnny Comes Marching Home")

The *P*s are marching into town. Hooray! Hooray!
The *P*s are marching in a great big *P* parade.
Some wear police hats and princess crowns.
Some hold pillows and march through town.
Oh, we're so glad the *P*s could come today.

The *P*s are marching into town. Hooray! Hooray!
Some are shaking pom-poms as they come our way.
Some wear plaid and some polka-dots.
Some have puppets and pans and pots.
Oh, we're so glad the *P*s could come today.

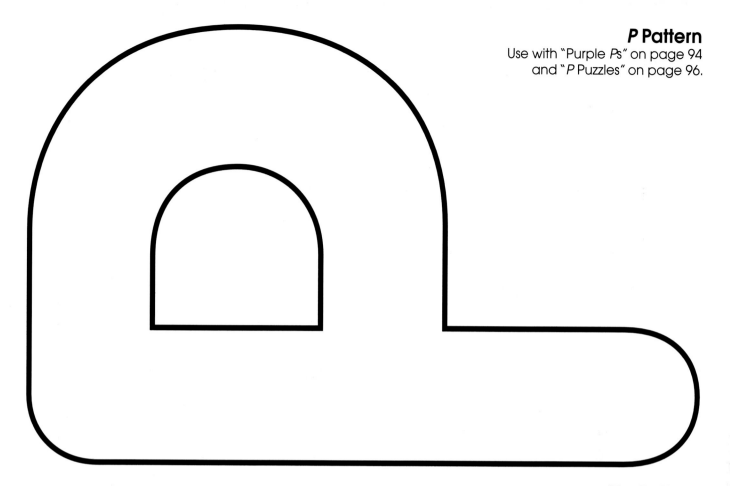

P Pattern
Use with "Purple Ps" on page 94
and "P Puzzles" on page 96.

Pig Pattern
Use with "Pig Puppets" on page 94.

The Letter Q

Quirky Qs

Spotlight the letter *Q* with this quirky activity. Copy and cut out the *Q* pattern on page 105 for each child. Also gather a supply of large craft feathers (quills) and set out shallow containers of colorful paint. Give each student a *Q* pattern and have him trace his finger over the letter as he says the letter name aloud. Then have him dip the pointed end of his quill into the paint and then use it to write an uppercase and a lowercase *Q* on his cutout. Have him redip the quill tip as needed and continue writing uppercase and lowercase *Q*s until a desired look is achieved.

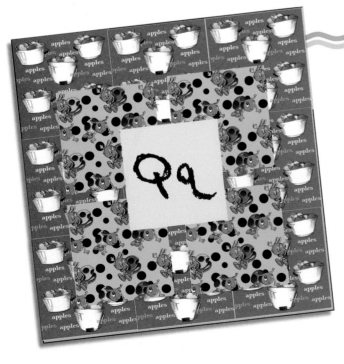

Quite a Nice Quilt!

This class-made quilt reinforces the letter *Q* quite nicely! To prepare, cut a few different kinds of colorful wrapping paper into three-inch squares. Also cut a nine-inch square and a three-inch square from construction paper for each child. If possible, share a real quilt with students. Then have each youngster choose several wrapping paper squares. Have her position these squares on the nine-inch square as desired and then glue them in place. Next, have her write an uppercase and a lower-case *Q* on the three-inch construction paper square and glue it to the center of her quilt block. Post the blocks on a wall to make a quilt and then add a length of lace around the edges to complete it.

Q's Friend U

Introduce youngsters to the partnership between the letters *Q* and *U* with this cute rhyme! To begin, read the provided rhyme to your youngsters. Then tell students that the letter *Q* is almost always followed by the letter *U,* and these two letters together make the /kw/ sound. Then give each child an index card labeled "Qu." Reread the rhyme and have each child hold up her card when she hears /kw/, the sound of the *qu* blend.

Q was very shy
Until he met *U.*
Now when *Q* goes out
He takes *U* too.

He still is very quiet,
But he has a lot of fun.
Now he is a quarterback
And questions everyone.

He even tried quilting
And baking quaint pies.
He is quite popular
And *U's* the reason why.

Quail Puppets

These lovely quails will certainly show your youngsters' creativity. Make a copy of the quail pattern (page 105) on white construction paper for each child and then cut the patterns out. Write the word *quail* on the board. (If possible, show students a picture of a quail.) Circle the *qu* blend and discuss it with students. Next, give each child a cutout and have him use crayons or washable markers to add facial features. Then provide students with shallow containers of glue and small craft feathers. Have each child dip the feathers in the glue and press them onto the cutout. When the projects are dry, tape a large craft stick to the back of each one to create a handle.

Quack for Q!

Students will go quackers over this literacy idea. Write the word *quack* on the board. Point out the *qu* blend and have students notice the /kw/ sound as they say the word. Then say several words (including some that start with *Q*). Ask students to quack like a duck one time when they hear a word that begins with *Q*. If the word begins with another letter, instruct them to sit quietly. For added fun, read aloud several books that feature the letter *Q* and encourage students to quack each time they hear a word that begins with the /q/ sound. Quack! Quack!

Asking Questions

Youngsters have all the answers with this simplified version of Twenty Questions! First, explain to students that some sentences tell things and some sentences ask things. The asking sentences are called questions. Write the word *questions* on the board. Then tell students that you're thinking of another word that starts with the /kw/ sound and challenge them to ask you up to ten questions about it. After you've answered the questions, have students guess the mystery word. Hmm, is it a person who wears a crown?

quick	quiet
rabbit	rabbit
horse	turtle
tiger	fish

Quick or Quiet?

Get your little ones thinking about quick and quiet animals. Head a two-column chart with "quick" and "quiet." Point out that both words start with the *qu* blend and have the same beginning sound. Also ask student volunteers to tell you what each word means. Then enlist students' help in naming animals and deciding whether they are quick, quiet, both, or neither. Write students' responses in the corresponding columns. Wow, a rabbit is quick and quiet!

Quick Q Moves

- Pretend to be quarterbacks throwing long passes.
- Waddle and quack like a duck.
- Chant "Jack, Be Nimble" and pretend to quickly jump over candlesticks.

Q Snacks

- Quaker oatmeal
- quick breads
- queen's tea party treats
- Quaker cereal

Q Café

Stock your dramatic-play area with items to create a *Q* café. Include empty food packages and play foods from the list above along with items such as a loaf pan for quick bread and a Quaker oatmeal box. Also set out materials for students to use to create signs, placemats, and menus.

The *Q* Café Song
(sung to the tune of "Jingle Bells")

Q café, *Q* café,
Full of special treats.
Let's go out and have some lunch.
It's just down the street.

Quick breads, quaint pies,
Quaker oatmeal too.
I just love the *Q* café
Which has good things to chew.

103

Q Parade

Plan a *Q* parade with your youngsters! Pick and choose from the following costume and prop ideas. Then teach the provided song and let the marching begin!

Costumes

- robes and crowns for queens
- quilts
- football jerseys for quarterbacks

Props

- feather quill pens
- quarters in a sealed jar
- Quaker oatmeal boxes
- cardboard question marks
- pictures of quails
- Q-tips cotton swabs

The *Q* Parade Song
(sung to the tune of "When Johnny Comes Marching Home")

The *Q*s are marching into town. Hooray! Hooray!
The *Q*s are marching in a great big *Q* parade.
Some carry quilts and some wear crowns.
Some walk quickly all around.
Oh, we're so glad the *Q*s could come today.

The *Q*s are marching into town. Hooray! Hooray!
Some are quacking as they march our way.
Some ask questions as they come.
Some shake quarters just for fun.
Oh, we're so glad the *Q*s could come today.

Quail Pattern
Use with "Quail Puppets" on page 101.

The Letter *R*

Rice *Rs*

Teach youngsters about the letter *R* with this small-group activity. Make a red construction paper copy of the *R* pattern on page 111 for each child and cut it out. Place a shallow bowl of glue, old paintbrushes, cotton swabs, and a box lid at a table. Gather a small group of students and discuss the letter *R*. Encourage students to say the beginning sound they hear in *rice* and *red*. Have each child spread glue on her cutout and then carefully sprinkle on rice. When the glue is dry, have her shake the excess rice into the box lid.

Rabbit Puppets

Twitch, twitch! Your little ones' noses will be twitching like a rabbit's when they make this sweet puppet. Make a construction paper copy of the rabbit pattern on page 111 for each child. Discuss with students the sound they hear at the beginning of *rabbit*. Then give each child a copy of the rabbit pattern, and have her color it and cut it out. Help each child tape a craft stick to the back of her rabbit to make a puppet.

Rectangular Robot

This radical robot will help youngsters shape up their letter *R* skills. Cut an assortment of rectangles from different colors of construction paper. To begin, discuss with students the sound they hear at the beginning of *robot* and ask them to name other words that begin with the same sound. Record student's ideas on a chart. Then give each child a sheet of construction paper and several rectangles. Ask him to arrange the shapes on the paper to create a robot and then glue them in place. Below his creation, help each child write or dictate a robot name that begins with the /r/ sound. Display students' work on a bulletin board titled "Our Rectangular Robots."

Ronnie Robot

106

Red Writing

Your little writers will radiate pride after completing this letter-formation activity. In advance, write an uppercase and a lowercase letter *R* on paper for each child to trace. On a chart or chalkboard, model for youngsters how to write the letter. Then give each child a sheet and ask her to trace the uppercase and lowercase letters with a red crayon or marker. Guide her to write one row of uppercase letters and one row of lowercase letters. Then display students' work on a board titled "Really Red Writers!"

Time to Sing

Replacing words in familiar tunes is a fun way to help students identify the /r/ sound. At circle time talk to youngsters about the beginning /r/ sound and help them list words that begin with the sound. Record students' ideas on a chart. Then lead your group in singing a song that features the /r/ sound, such as "Row, Row, Row Your Boat." Sing the song again, replacing a word in the song with a word from the chart. For example, you might sing, "Row, row, row your raft." Repeat the song several times, using a different word from the chart each time. As different words are substituted and the song gets sillier, students will have no problem remembering the /r/ sound. Really!

Row, row, row, your raft.

raft
rocket
rope
radio

Ready? Action!

Youngsters' reactions to this movement activity offer them practice identifying words with the initial consonant *R*. In advance, label index cards with actions that begin with the /r/ sound, such as *run, row, rake, reach, rotate, rise, ride,* and *rest.* To begin, read each card to your group and lead them in performing the corresponding action. Then mix up the cards and ask one child to choose a card. Whisper the word to her and have her perform the action for her classmates to guess. Repeat the activity so that each child has a turn.

Ribbon Reinforcement

Reinforce the /r/ sound with this ribbon sequencing activity. Cut several different lengths of wide ribbon. Gather a small group of students, show them a length of ribbon and discuss the beginning /r/ sound. Then help students arrange the ribbons in order from shortest to longest. Challenge youngsters to name a word that begins with the /r/ sound as you point to each ribbon.

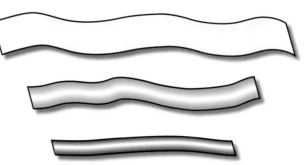

Rulers Rule!

Introduce measurement skills as students make a letter-sound connection. Show your group a ruler and tell them that it is used to measure objects. Then have each child say the beginning /r/ sound heard in *ruler*. Give each child a ruler and invite her to explore measuring the lengths of different classroom objects. Encourage each child to state her findings.

Really Counting

Counting real objects into sets is just right for little ones! In advance, obtain sets of different items that begin with the letter *R* such as racecars, rubber snakes, and stuffed rabbits. Mix up the items and then, during circle time, show your group one item from each set. Discuss with them the beginning /r/ sound of each item. Then spread the toys in the middle of your circle and help youngsters sort them into sets by type. Encourage students to count and then compare the sets. Then help them decide which set has more and which set has less. Place the toys at a center for each child to have the opportunity to count and sort.

Radical *R* Moves

- Run in place.
- Pretend to blast like a rocket.
- Pretend to ride a horse.
- Hop like a rabbit.
- Pretend to rake leaves.
- Jump over a rope.

R Snacks

- rice pudding
- rolls
- relish
- raspberry gelatin
- ravioli
- ranch dip and vegetables

R Café

Stock your dramatic-play area with items to create an *R* café. Include empty food packages and play foods from the list above. Also set out materials for your students to use to create signs, placemats, and menus.

The *R* Café Song
(sung to the tune of "Yankee Doodle")

The *R* café is new in town
With *R* foods—what a treat!
Let's go down and check it out
And order food to eat.

Red potatoes and pot roast,
Raspberry gelatin too.
Rolls, rice pudding, and ravioli,
Waiting just for you.

R Parade

Plan an *R* parade with youngsters! Pick and choose from the following costume and prop ideas. Then teach the provided song and let the marching begin!

Costumes

- ribbons

- rainbow-colored scarves

- red clothes

- raincoats and hats

- rubber boots

- rabbit ears
  (Attach construction paper rabbit ear shapes to a headband.)

Props

- rattles

- rain sticks

- stuffed rabbits

- rulers

- toy rockets

- radios

The *R* Parade Song
*(sung to the tune
"When Johnny Comes Marching Home")*

The *R*s are marching into town. Hooray! Hooray!
The *R*s are marching in a great big *R* parade.
Some shake rattles, and some wear rings.
Some play rock and roll as they sing.
Oh, we're so glad the *R*s could come today.

The *R*s are marching into town. Hooray! Hooray!
Some are roller-skating as they come our way.
Some wear raincoats; some twirl ropes.
Some carry rockets on a float.
Oh, we're so glad the *R*s could come today.

Rabbit Pattern
Use with "Rabbit Puppets" on page 106.

The Letter S

A Special S

These swell activities are just what you need to get your little ones familiar with the letter *S*. Enlarge a copy of the *S* pattern on page 117; then copy it onto white construction paper for each child and cut it out. Choose one of the following ideas for embellishing the cutout, and set up the needed supplies. Give each child an *S* pattern and have him say its sound before explaining the art idea and how it relates to the letter *S*.

Then assist students as necessary to complete their *S* masterpieces.

- Make squiggles with glue; then sprinkle sand over them.
- Hole-punch colored construction paper and then glue the resulting "spots" on the letter cutout.
- Use a star-shaped rubber stamp to add a stellar design.
- Paint the shape green and add wiggle eyes stickers and a red felt tongue to make an S-shaped snake.
- Add snowflake stickers for a snowy scene.

Seal Puppets

These slick seal puppets will help students balance fun with recognizing the /s/ sound. Make a construction paper cutout of the seal pattern on page 117 for each child. Also prepare a batch of slick paint by tinting evaporated milk with blue food coloring. Have each child paint his seal with the slick paint. When the paint is dry, tape a craft stick to the back of each seal to make a puppet. Have students move their seals so they look as though they're swimming as they say the /s/ sound. Splash!

Splendid Sunflowers

Plant some *S* awareness with these stunning sunflowers. To make a sunflower, a student paints a paper plate brown. When the paint has dried, he uses a black marker to write the letter *S* on the plate and glues yellow construction paper petals along the perimeter. To make seeds, he presses a pencil eraser onto a black stamp pad and then onto the plate repeatedly to make seeds. Showcase these sunny flowers on a bulletin board titled "*S* Is 'Sun-sational'!"

Sandpaper S

The sense of touch helps the letter *S* take shape for youngsters. Cut several *S* shapes from sandpaper (pattern on page 117). Place the cutouts at a center. During a center visit, a student traces over the letters with her finger and then writes an *S* on a sheet of paper. Or, for a textured twist, she uses a crayon (with the paper wrapping removed) to make a rubbing of the sandpaper *S* on a sheet of white paper.

Sally saw _____ at the seashore.

seaweed

Seashore Sentences

Read aloud the following sentence to your students: "Sally saw _____ at the seashore." Then write it on a chart. Create a picture card for each of the following *S* items, adding "a" or "the" as necessary: seagull, seaweed, sand, starfish, sailboat, submarine, seal, and sun. During circle time, have a child take a picture card and identify the picture. Then have all students say the picture name, and lead them to conclude that it begins with the /s/ sound. Finally, tape the picture on the blank and read aloud the resulting sentence. Encourage your little ones to repeat the sentence. Continue in this manner until all of the cards have been used. That's a lot of *S* words!

Sea Scene

This activity not only features words that begin with /s/, but it also helps students practice positional words. Draw a simple sea scene on your chalkboard as shown. Show your little ones a picture of a sea-related item. (Use the cards from "Seashore Sentences" on this page.) After a student has named the item, have him identify whether it would be found *in, on, over,* or *beside* the sea. If desired, tape the card in the appropriate spot on the chalkboard drawing.

sailboat

S Store

Encourage communication and further exploration of the letter *S* by creating an *S* store in your classroom. Stock the store only with things whose names begin with the /s/ sound. Be sure to include sandals, seashells, silk scarves, socks, spoons, sunglasses, etc. Provide supplies for signs to advertise these *S* specials; then let the shopping spree begin!

Ss for the Senses

Continue your emphasis of the letter *S* and incorporate a study of the five senses. Gather sandpaper (touch), a strawberry-scented item such as lotion or soap (smell), syrup (taste), and saxophone music (played on a CD or tape player—hearing). Also write a large letter *S* on a chalkboard (sight). Discuss each of the senses and introduce its corresponding item so that students can experience it with the appropriate sense. For example, cover students' eyes as they taste or feel items. Then have them discuss how each special sense helped them to identify the item. Also say each item name aloud and have students listen for the /s/ sound.

Sets of Six

What number begins with the same sound as *seashell?* Six, of course. Place 12 seashells in a center and encourage students to count sets of six. What a great way to provide number practice while highlighting the /s/ sound! But don't stop there! Add 14 socks to the center and challenge students to count sets of seven socks. Splendid!

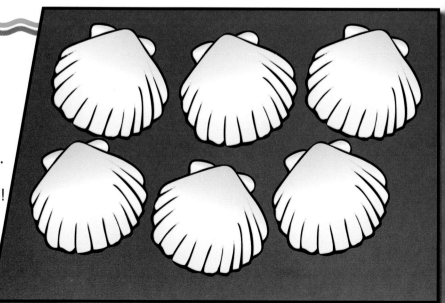

Silly *S* Moves

- skip
- slide
- slip
- somersault
- stand
- sweep
- swim
- swing

S Snacks

- soups
- salads
- sandwiches
- stew
- s'mores
- strawberries
- spinach
- squash
- spaghetti
- seafood

S Café

Stock your dramatic-play area with items to create an *S* café. Include empty food packages and play foods from the list above along with items such as spoons, stools, spatulas, and salt shakers. Also set out materials for students to use to create signs, placemats, and menus.

The *S* Café Song
(sung to the tune of "Take Me Out to the Ballgame")

Let's go down to the *S* café.
We'll have some strawberry pie.
Let's go down to the *S* café.
They have *S* meals in every size:
Salad, spaghetti, and seafood,
Soups and sandwiches to name a few.
For it's one great day to eat *S* meals
At the *S* café!

S Parade

Plan an *S* parade with your youngsters! Pick and choose from the following costume and prop ideas. Then teach the provided song and let the marching begin!

Costumes

- socks
- suits
- sailor hats
- soldier hats
- skirts
- sweaters
- snowsuits
- slippers
- silk scarves

Props

- sunglasses
- spoons
- skates
- sleds
- sunflowers
- toy sailboats
- silver star headbands
  (Attach silver star stickers to tagboard headbands and size a headband to fit each child; then staple.)

The *S* Parade Song
(sung to the tune of "When Johnny Comes Marching Home")

The *S*s are marching into town. Hooray! Hooray!
The *S*s are marching in a great big *S* parade.
Some wear snowsuits and pull their sleds.
Some wear silver stars on their heads.
Oh, we're so glad the *S*s could come today.

The *S*s are marching into town. Hooray! Hooray!
They've put on suits and silky scarves to march our way.
Some sing songs and swing and sway.
Some skate in socks all the way.
Oh, we're so glad the *S*s could come today.

S Pattern
Use with "A Special *S*" on page 112
and "Sandpaper *S*"
on page 113.

Seal Pattern
Use with "Seal Puppets" on
page 112.

The Letter T

Terrific Ts

These terrific Ts show the creativity of each of your little ones. Make a tagboard copy of the T pattern on page 123 for each child. Have each youngster cut out his T and then use one or more of the suggestions below to decorate it. Have youngsters share their Ts with classmates, emphasizing the /t/ sound each time they name a decoration.

- Glue on short pieces of tinsel.
- Attach pieces of colorful tape.
- Make tire tracks by dipping a toy car in paint and then rolling the tires across the paper.
- Attach tulip stickers.
- Use turkey rubber stamps to make prints.

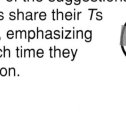

Turtle Puppets

Youngsters make a splash writing Ts on these cute turtle puppets! In advance, make a tagboard copy of the turtle pattern on page 123 for each child. Cut several shades of green tissue paper into one-inch squares to make a large supply. Give each youngster a turtle pattern and have her cut it out. Instruct her to color the turtle head, legs, and tail as desired. Then have her glue tissue paper squares to the turtle shell. After the glue is dry, encourage her to write the letter T on several sections of her turtle's shell. Then help each child make a handle for her puppet by taping a jumbo craft stick to the back of her turtle. Invite each child to use her puppet to point to T things around the room.

Tons of Tulips

Tiny tulips bloom when students work together to make this delightful display! To prepare, cut sponges into tulip shapes. Hot-glue a spool to each tulip sponge to make a stamper as shown. Tape a long length of bulletin board paper to a table. Invite several children at a time to visit the table. Provide each youngster with a stamper and access to paint. Have him dip his stamper in paint and then make prints on the paper. When the paint is dry, invite each child to help add a stem and two leaves to each tulip—in the shape of a lowercase T, of course!

118

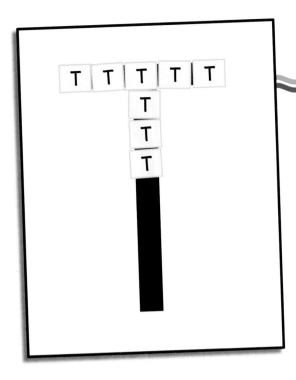

Finding Ts

This activity will have youngsters recognizing the letter *T* and thinking of words that start with it! To prepare, write the letter *T* on several sticky notes. Also label several notes with letters other than *T.* Hide the notes around your classroom. Then, on a length of bulletin board paper, write a large *T.* Have each child search the room for notes with *Ts* on them. Each time one is found, have the child say a *T* word as she positions her note on the large *T.* Have youngsters continue searching until all the *Ts* are found.

T Stories

Travel to the library to look for popular children's books and folk tales that have *T* words in them. As you read the stories to youngsters, emphasize the *T* words you come across. Have students make a *T* with their fingers every time they hear a word that begins with the letter *T.* Easy!

T Tours

Little ones will be eager to set up *T* tours in your classroom with this idea. Have a group of students collect from your room items whose names begin with the letter *T.* Have them place a few *T* items on each of several different tables. Position a different child at each tour table to be its tour guide. Lead the remainder of your students by each table and have its tour guide talk about the *T* items on the table. On another day, have students switch roles to become new tour guides or new tourists.

Talking on Telephones

Ring! Ring! Telephones are the answer to practicing the /t/ sound. Put two toy telephones and a stack of picture cards, many of which show items whose names begin with T, at a center. Encourage a pair of youngsters to talk to each other on the phones. Have one child flip through the cards and say each picture's name. Instruct the other child to make the /t/ sound when she hears a word that begins with T and say "beep" when she hears a word that does not begin with T. After going through the stack of cards, have youngsters switch roles and play again. Encourage students to practice good phone manners while playing the game. Thank you and goodbye!

/t/

/t/, /t/, Tiger

For a growling good time that focuses on the letter T, make these cute tigers. Provide each child with a paper plate (the uncoated kind) and access to black and orange paint. Have him brush stripes on his plate. With each stroke, instruct him to say, "/t/, /t/, tiger!" When the paint is dry, invite him to add construction paper facial features and ears. Roar!

Toes on a T

Little ones will love to dip their toes in paint to help make this T poster! To prepare, write a large uppercase T on a 12" x 18" sheet of construction paper for each child. Pour paint in a pan large enough for students to step in. (Prepare a tub of warm, soapy water and have towels on hand for a quick cleanup.) Help each child place one foot in the paint and then position it on her paper to make prints on the T. When the paint is dry, have her write uppercase Ts on her big-toe prints and lowercase Ts on the others!

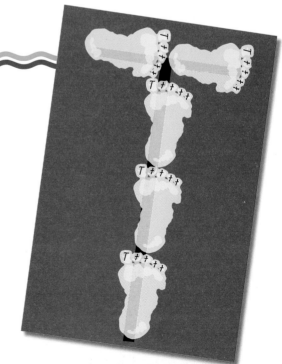

Trendy *T* Moves

- Tiptoe across the room.
- Pretend to talk on the telephone.
- Stand as tall as you can.
- Growl like a tiger.
- Pretend to brush your teeth.
- Crawl under a table.
- Touch your toes.

T Snacks

- tea
- toast
- tuna
- tacos
- tomatoes
- turkey
- tortilla chips
- tapioca pudding
- tarts

T Café

Stock your dramatic-play area with items to create a *T* café. Include empty food packages and play foods from the list above along with items such as tablecloths, tables, teapots, pie tins, and tea towels. Also set out materials for students to use to create signs, placemats, and menus.

The *T* Café Song
(sung to the tune of "Are You Sleeping?")

T café, *T* café—
Special treats, good to eat.
Tacos, tomatoes, and tuna,
Tea, toast, and tarts—
Special treats, tasty to eat.

T Parade

Plan a *T* parade with your youngsters! Pick and choose from the following costume and prop ideas. Then teach the provided song and let the marching begin!

Costumes

- clothing with tassels

- turkey feathers

- T-shirts

- top hats

- tap shoes or ballet toe shoes

- tennis clothes

- tennis shoes

- tinsel headbands
  (Glue two-inch lengths of tinsel to headbands. After the glue is dry, size the headbands to fit.)

Props

- tambourines

- towels

- tennis rackets

- tennis balls

- telephones

- teddy bears

- plastic teacups

- plastic teapots

- tops

The *T* Parade Song
(sung to the tune of "When Johnny Comes Marching Home")

The *T*s are marching into town. Hooray! Hooray!
The *T*s are marching in a great big *T* parade.
Some wear T-shirts and tennis shoes.
Some have teacups and teapots too.
Oh, we're so glad the *T*s could come today.

The *T*s are marching into town. Hooray! Hooray!
Some shake tambourines as they come our way.
Some have telephones and tennis balls.
Some have teddy bears three feet tall.
Oh, we're so glad the *T*s could come today.

T Pattern

Use with "Terrific *Ts*" on page 118.

Turtle Pattern

Use with "Turtle Puppets" on page 118.

The Letter U

Unusual *U* Prints

What part of a vegetable looks just like the letter *U?* The cut end of a celery stalk! Enlarge a copy of the *U* pattern (page 129) and make a white construction paper copy for each child. Cut several three-inch lengths of celery and place them in your art center along with shallow pans of tempera paint. Invite a small group of children to the center, and show them a piece of celery. Explain that the end of the celery is shaped exactly like the letter *U*. Then give each youngster a *U* pattern. Have him dip the cut end of a celery piece into the paint and make prints on and around the *U*. After the paint is dry, display these unusual *U*s in your classroom.

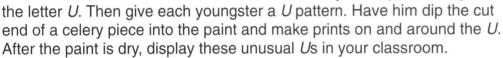

Umbrella Puppets

Rainy days aren't so gloomy with these colorful umbrella puppets! Give each child an enlarged white construction paper copy of the umbrella pattern (page 129). Encourage her to paint the pattern with watercolors. If the papers curl when dry, place them under a stack of books overnight to flatten them. Invite each youngster to cut out the pattern and then use a marker to draw a face on the umbrella. Then help each child tape a jumbo craft stick to the back of the umbrella to make a puppet. Have students hold their umbrella puppets while practicing the letter *U* and its long and short sounds.

Umbrellas in the Rain

These little umbrellas look lovely with this stormy blue and purple sky! Cut a supply of blue and purple tissue paper into squares (dark-colored tissue paper works best for this activity). To begin, present a real umbrella. Have students say the word *umbrella* and listen carefully for the short *U* sound. Next, a youngster randomly arranges several tissue paper squares on a sheet of 9" x 12" white construction paper. She uses a paintbrush to carefully brush water over the tissue paper. When the tissue paper is dry, she peels off the squares to reveal a colorful stormy sky. Then each youngster flattens a cupcake liner and cuts it in half. She glues each half to the paper to resemble an umbrella; then she glues a mini craft stick handle to each one.

U Puzzles

With these vivid *U* puzzles, youngsters practice sorting skills as well as spatial skills! Enlarge a copy of the *U* pattern on page 129. Then make a construction paper copy in each of the following colors: red, blue, and yellow. Cut the patterns into large puzzle pieces and then place the puzzles at a center. A child visits the center, sorts the pieces by color, and then assembles each *U* puzzle!

U Search

Under a book! Under a desk! Youngsters search for *U* cards with this fun idea—and each one is under an object in your classroom! In advance, make a class supply of *U* cards plus a few extras. Before children arrive for the day, place each card under an object in your classroom. To begin, review the shape and sound of the letter *U* with your youngsters. Then have them repeat the word *under* and listen carefully for the short *U* sound. Next, encourage each child to look under objects in the classroom to find a *U* card. When each child finds a card, have him sit in your circle-time area. Then ask each student to share where he found his card, using the word *under* in his reply.

U Shapes

What is squishy, bendable, and excellent for forming the letter *U*? Why, play dough, of course! Place a supply of colorful play dough at a table. If desired, also provide several laminated copies of the *U* pattern (page 129) for reference. Invite a small group of children to the center. Have each youngster roll the play dough into a log shape. Then encourage her to bend the log to form the letter *U*. Finally, have her trace the *U* with her finger and say its name.

125

Over and Under

What might be found over and under an umbrella? Your youngsters decide with this fun position-word game! In advance, make a supply of picture cards showing objects that might be found over and under an umbrella (see the suggestions given). Draw a large umbrella on a sheet of chart paper and post the paper in your circle-time area. To begin, have youngsters repeat the words *under* and *umbrella* and listen carefully for the short *U* sound. Then present a picture card and have the students decide whether the object pictured would most likely be found over or under an umbrella. Invite a child to tape the card in the corresponding location on the chart paper. Continue in a similar fashion until each card has been placed on the paper.

Picture suggestions: raindrops, a rainbow, a cloud, a bird, an airplane, a child, grass, a flower, a dog, the sidewalk

Up, Up, and Away

Have little ones put on their thinking caps and tell you about things that go up! Draw an outline of a rocket ship on a sheet of chart paper and display it in your circle-time area. Explain that a rocket ship can go up. Have students repeat the word *up* and listen for the short *U* sound. Then encourage them to pretend to be a rocket ship taking off into outer space. Next, have little ones suggest other things that can go up. After writing each appropriate idea on the rocket ship, encourage little ones to mimic the movement of that object.

Uniforms Aplenty

Provide long *U* reinforcement with this class book, which is sure to be uniformly enjoyed by all! Write the word *uniform* on your board and have youngsters locate the letter *U.* Then invite students to share the names of workers or groups that wear uniforms as you write each one under the word. After several ideas are written, give each student a sheet of 12" x 18" white construction paper. Invite her to draw a person in the uniform of her choice. Write the person's profession or title under the picture. Then bind the pages together with a cover titled "So Many Uniforms!" Finally, read the completed book to your youngsters.

Unbelievable *U* Moves

- Pretend to play the ukulele.
- Pretend to hold an umbrella during a windy rainstorm.
- Pretend to swim underwater.
- Pretend to unwrap a gift.
- Pretend to unlock a door with a giant key.

U Snacks

- upside-down cake
- celery sticks and dip (The cut end of each piece of celery resembles the letter *U*.)
- any snack that youngsters must unwrap

U Café

Stock your dramatic-play area with items to create a *U* café. Include empty food packages and play foods from the list above along with items such as utensils and foil to practice wrapping and unwrapping food. Also set out materials for students to use to create signs, placemats, and menus.

The *U* Café Song
(sung to the tune of "Down by the Station")

Let's go out to eat
At the *U* café.
Sitting under umbrellas
All in a row.

See the upside-down cake
Just out of the oven.
Let's have a big piece
Before we go!

Plan a *U* parade with your youngsters! Pick and choose from the following costume and prop ideas. Then teach the provided song and let the marching begin!

Costumes

- sports uniforms, such as softball or T-ball

- Girl Scout or Boy Scout uniforms

- uniforms for various workers, such as a police officer, a nurse, or a firefighter

Props

- umbrellas

- utensils

- toy ukuleles

- unicorn stuffed animals

- university pennants

- unicorn horns
  (To make a horn, brush glue on a colorful party hat and then sprinkle glitter over the glue.)

The *U* Parade Song
(sung to the tune of "When Johnny Comes Marching Home")

The *U*s are marching into town. Hooray! Hooray!
The *U*s are marching in a great big *U* parade.
Some wear colorful unicorn horns.
Some have umbrellas in case of a storm.
Oh, we're so glad the *U*s could come today.

The *U*s are marching into town. Hooray! Hooray!
The *U*s are marching in a great big *U* parade.
There are uniforms and utensils to see
And a person playing the ukulele.
Oh, we're so glad the *U*s could come today.

U Pattern

Use with "Unusual *U* Prints" on page 124 and "*U* Puzzles" and "*U* Shapes" on page 125.

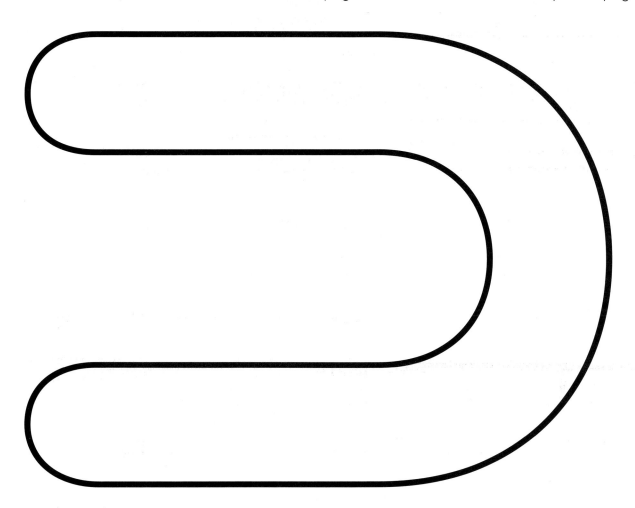

Umbrella Pattern

Use with "Umbrella Puppets" on page 124.

The Letter V

Vivid Vs

*V*s come to life in this fine-motor activity that helps develop letter-sound awareness! Enlarge a copy of the *V* pattern on page 135 and make a copy on white construction paper for each child. Provide brightly colored, washable ink pads and vegetables—such as peppers, carrots, and celery—that have been sliced in half. Write the word *vegetable* and say it out loud. Circle the beginning letter and discuss the letter-sound correspondence. Then give each child a pattern and have him stamp vegetables prints on it. As he does this, encourage him to softly say other words that begin like *vegetable*. When the pattern is dry, have him cut out the letter. *Valentine, velvet, violins,* and lots and lots of *veggies!*

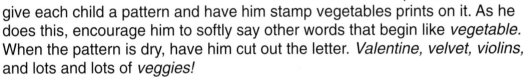

Violet Visors

Get into the *V* spirit with a vivacious violet visor! For each child, cut a nine-inch white paper plate as shown, and gather violet glitter pens and assorted violet stickers. Show students a container of violet paint. Write the word *violet* on the board and point out its beginning letter. Have each child paint his plate violet and let it dry. Then invite him to decorate it with the glitter pens and stickers. Encourage him to softly say the letter *V* and make the /v/ sound as he works. Add letter-formation practice by inviting him to write *V*s on his visor. When the visor is dry, cut ¾-inch slits along the cut edge and fold them up. Help him punch a hole on each outer edge of the visor. Tie a length of violet ribbon onto each hole. Then help him tie the visor to fit. Looking good!

Valentine Collage

Build letter-sound awareness with these heartwarming collages! In advance, cut a supply of heart shapes from various colors of tissue paper. Also provide scraps and strips of tissue paper. Give each child a sheet of white construction paper, access to an old paintbrush and water-thinned glue, and the tissue paper cutouts. Invite her to brush glue over her construction paper and then cover the glue with tissue paper cutouts. Encourage her to overlap the cutouts to create interesting colors and shapes. When the glue is dry, help her fold the paper and cut out a large heart. Help her write "Be My Valentine" on the back of the collage, and point out the letter *V*. Invite her to make the /v/ sound and trace over the *V* with her finger several times. Then have her take the valentine collage home to someone special.

Be My Valentine

Be My Valentine

Secret messages are lots of fun to find and fun to read too! Cut a variety of violet construction paper hearts. Use a silver pen to program each with a simple message that incorporates the word *valentine.* Then hide a few valentines in your classroom each day. When a child finds one, take a minute to read aloud the message and reinforce the letter-sound connection.

V Words

Vocabulary is the big winner in this matching game! Write and illustrate the words shown that begin with *V* on large index cards. Also program sentence strips with the sentence starters shown. Put the strips in a pocket chart and turn the cards facedown on a nearby table. Gather a group of students and explain that one card goes with each sentence starter very well; the others may sound silly. Then invite a child to select a card and identify it. Read aloud the first sentence and ask him to decide if the word is a good match. If it is, he places the card in the pocket, and you read the completed sentence. If it's not a good match, read the second sentence, then the third, and so on until he finds the best match. Then have another child select a card and repeat the matching game. I will ride in a vegetable? That's silly!

Vet Visit

Do your youngsters know that there are also *V* occupations? It's true—a veterinarian is a pet's best friend! Invite a local veterinarian to visit your classroom and describe her job. You may wish to provide a stuffed animal for her to examine so children can see her in action. Afterward, enlist student help to write a thank-you letter to the veterinarian on chart paper. Invite volunteers to circle all the *V*s. Then revisit those words and reinforce the letter-sound connection. Finally, copy the letter onto notepaper and mail it to the vet. What a great visit!

Dear Dr. Vincente,
Thank you for visiting our class when we learned about the letter V! We learned a lot about how veterinarians care for animals. Fluffy feels good now. The animals are lucky to have you make them feel better.
Love,
Ms. Warren's Class

Veronica   Alix   Jamal   TelVon   Sam
Shanita   Zain   Sarajane

131

How Many Vs?

Letter-formation, counting, and fine-motor skills are rolled into this very fine play dough activity! Give each child a portion of play dough, and have him roll it into a snake. Show him how to pinch off a length and then form it into a *V*. Encourage him to make as many *V*s as possible with his dough. Then help him count all the *V*s. Very, very good job!

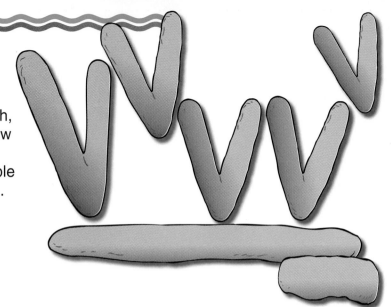

The Velvet Touch

Soft, elegant velvet is a touching way to reinforce the /v/ sound. Gather four or five different fabric scraps and a piece of velvet. Invite students to feel the velvet scrap and compare it with the other fabrics. Encourage each child to take a turn completing the sentence "Velvet feels…" Then put all the fabrics into a pillowcase (or feely bag) and invite youngsters to try to identify the velvet by touch. As a child touches each fabric, have him softly say the /v/ sound. When he's found the velvet, have him pull it from the bag while saying, "Velvet!"

Veggie Puzzles

Here's a bumper crop of *V* awareness! In advance, duplicate the vegetable basket pattern on page 135 to make a supply for a center. Color the vegetable baskets as desired; then puzzle-cut each to make a unique matching pair as shown. Mix up the puzzle pieces and have a child put each pair together so that each puzzle has an uppercase and a lowercase *V*.

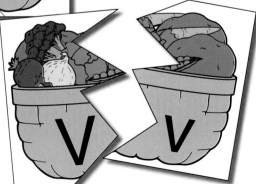

Valuable V Moves

- Play volleyball with a soft nylon ball.
- Pretend to play a violin.
- Pretend to fly like geese in a *V* formation.
- Use your body to make a *V*. Then make one with a partner.

V Snacks

- vegetable soup
- cut up vegetables and dip
- vanilla yogurt
- vanilla wafers
- vanilla ice cream

V Café

Stock your dramatic-play area with items to create a *V* café. Include empty food packages and play foods from the list above along with items such as vinyl tablecloths and vegetable bins and brushes. Also set out materials for students to use to create signs, placemats, and menus.

The *V* Café Song
(sung to the tune of "Jingle Bells")

V café, *V* café,
Full of special treats.
Let's go have some lunch.
It's just down the street.

Vegetable soup, vanilla wafers,
That is what I'll eat.
I just love the *V* café
With all its *V* treats.

V Parade

Plan a *V* Parade with your students! Pick and choose from the following costume and prop ideas. Then teach the provided song and let the marching begin!

Costumes

- veils

- visors

- velvet clothing

- veterinarian coats

- Velcro brand fastened shoes

- vests
  (Open a brown paper grocery bag. Cut one center panel in half vertically and then cut a round neck opening in the bottom panel. Cut an arm hole in each side panel. Decorate the vest with crayons, markers, and assorted craft supplies.)

Props

- plastic vegetables

- volleyballs

- toy vehicles

- plastic vases

- artificial violets

- empty video boxes

- valentines

The *V* Parade Song
*(sung to the tune of
When Johnny Comes Marching Home")*

The *V*s are marching into town. Hooray! Hooray!
The *V*s are marching in a great big *V* parade.
Some wear vests and Velcro shoes.
Some carry videos and vegetables too.
Oh, we're so glad the *V*s could come today.

The *V*s are marching into town. Hooray! Hooray!
Some are holding volleyballs as they come our way.
Some carry violets and long green vines.
Some have velvet and valentines.
Oh, we're so glad the *V*s could come today.

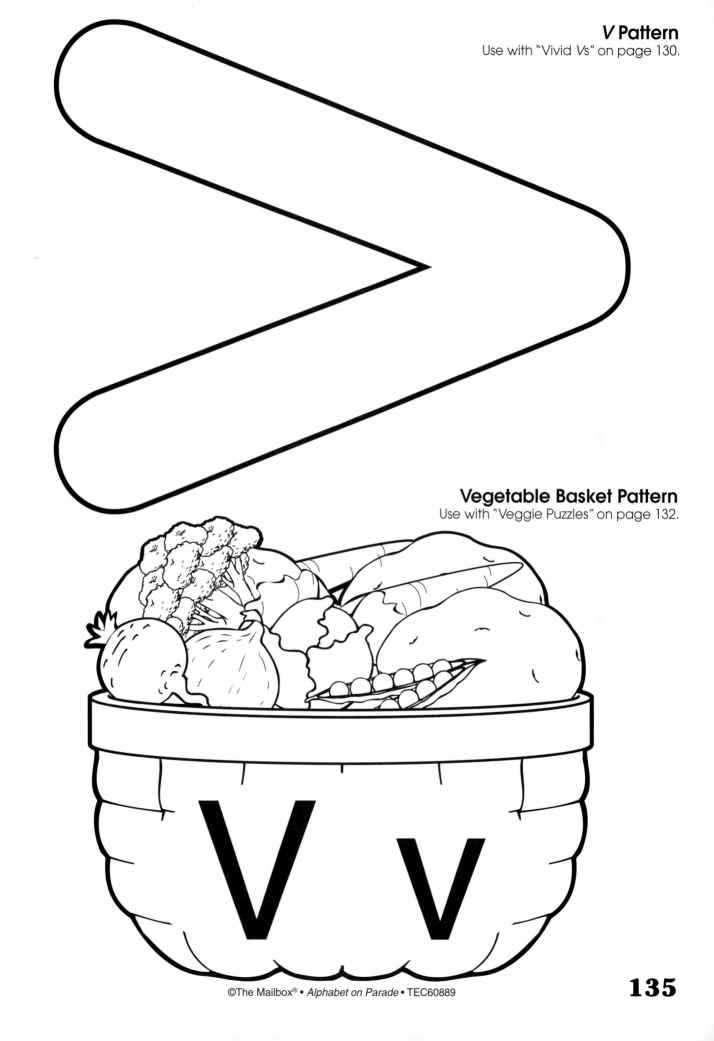

V Pattern
Use with "Vivid *Vs*" on page 130.

Vegetable Basket Pattern
Use with "Veggie Puzzles" on page 132.

V v

The Letter W

Wiggly Worm Ws

Develop letter-sound awareness with these wacky worm Ws! In advance, make a copy of the W pattern on page 141 onto white construction paper for each child; then cut it out. Provide brightly colored markers or crayons. Encourage a child to draw and color worms on his cutout. As he does this, encourage him to softly say other words that begin like *worm.* Wiggle, wiggle!

Walrus Puppets

What marine animal has long tusks and a name that begins with *W?* Why, a walrus, of course! Duplicate onto brown construction paper the walrus pattern on page 141 to make a class supply. Cut out the walrus shapes and give one to each child. Have him add facial features with markers. Provide each child with two white craft foam tusks and six two-inch white yarn whiskers. Help him glue the features onto the walrus's face. When the glue is dry, turn over the walrus, write "[Child's Name]'s Walrus" on the back, and read it aloud to him. Point out the letter *W* and invite him to say the word *walrus,* listening for the /w/ sound. Then tape a jumbo craft stick to the back of the cutout to make a puppet.

Watercolor Paintings

Brush up on letter-sound awareness while creating an artistic masterpiece! Give each child a sheet of white construction paper, access to a paintbrush, and watercolor paints. Write the word *watercolor* on the board and say it aloud. Point out the letter *W,* and have each child say the word and the /w/ sound several times. Then invite her to paint pictures of items whose names begin like the word *watercolor.* Encourage her to fill her paper with a few W items. When the paint is dry, assist each student in labeling her items. Then display the masterpieces for a wonderful wall of *W!*

136

Found a Worm
(sung to the tune of "Found a Peanut")

Found a worm. Found a worm.

Found a worm just now.

Just now I found a worm.

It was wiggling on a _____.

web   wagon

Found a Worm

Here's a cheerful little ditty about a worm who wiggles over lots of *W* items to help your youngsters develop letter-sound awareness. In advance, make a set of picture word cards of items whose names begin with *W,* such as a window, watch, web, wolf, wallet, window, wall, and watermelon. Next, copy the song shown onto chart paper. Teach students the song. Then invite a child to choose a card and identify the picture. Sing the song, using that word to fill in the blank at the end. Repeat the activity several times with different *W* words.

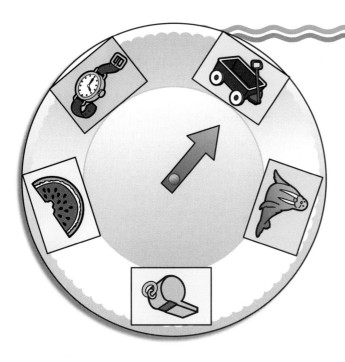

Story Word Wheel

Talk about a good story—this interactive wheel will whet your childrens' appetites for *W!* Cut out a variety of magazine pictures of objects whose names begin with *W.* Glue them to the rim of a paper plate. When the glue is dry, add a narrow tagboard arrow attached to the plate's center with a brass fastener. Start a story about Wanda and Willy. Pause and invite a child to spin the wheel. Have her identify the *W* picture indicated and incorporate it into the story. Continue in this manner until each child has had a chance to spin the wheel.

Writing *W*s

Try a few of these creative options to build letter-formation skills!
- Bend pipe cleaners into *W*s.
- Write *W*s with sidewalk chalk on a paved surface.
- Paint *W*s with water on an outside wall.
- Write *W*s in crayon on light paper; then brush a watercolor wash over top. The crayon will peek through!

Wild Versus Tame

Here's an animal classification game that also reinforces letter-sound awareness. Gather students and discuss the meanings of *wild* and *tame.* Then ask students to make a *W* with three fingers when they hear you name a wild animal. Ask students to quietly hold their hands in their laps when they hear you name a tame animal. Slowly name a variety of animals and watch for the appropriate responses.

Weighing In

If incorporating *W* into measurement has been weighing on your mind, bring out a balance scale, and let's get to work! Collect a variety of *W* items, such as plastic worms, watches, wallets, a bottle of water, a plush walrus, a plush wolf, a block of wax, and so forth. Invite a child to name two items to compare and load each onto the balance scale. Then have him tell which *W* item weighs more. Continue in this manner until each child has had a turn. Wow! The wolf weighs more than the wax!

Water Exploration

Want to explore the letter-sound connection of *W*s? Just add water! Fill your water table and add a plastic measuring cup and several different-size containers. Gather a group of children and have each child say the word *water* aloud several times and identify the beginning sound. Next, ask a child to predict how many cups of water a particular container will hold. Then help her measure that amount of water into the container. How close was her prediction? Would she need more or less water to fill the container another time? Discuss the results; then repeat the activity with another child and container.

Wonderful W Moves

- Wiggle your arms and legs and then your whole body.
- Waddle like a duck.
- Pretend to wash windows.
- Pretend to flap wings.
- Walk in different wacky ways.

W Snacks

- waffles
- seedless watermelon
- wafer cookies
- Waldorf salad
- cups of iced water

W Café

Stock your dramatic-play area with items to create a *W* café. Include empty food packages and play foods from the list above along with items such as waxed paper sheets, waiter aprons, and wiping cloths. Also set out materials for students to use to create signs, placemats, and menus.

The *W* Café Song
(sung to the tune of "Yankee Doodle")

The *W* café is new in town
With *W* foods—what a treat.
Let's go down and check it out
And order food to eat.

Watermelon and waffles,
Wafer cookies too.
Waldorf salad and iced water
All fresh just for you.

W Parade

Plan a *W* parade with your children. Pick and choose from the following costumes and prop ideas. Then teach the provided song and let the marching begin!

Costumes

- wigs

- wizard hats

- wings

- western clothes

- water gear

- watches

Props

- wagons

- washcloths

- wallets

- water toys

- wooden toys

- wishing wands
  (Cut a three-inch star shape from tagboard. Glue the star to a jumbo craft stick to make a wand. Use crayons, markers, and assorted craft supplies to decorate the wishing wand. Then tape on lengths of curling ribbon.)

The *W* Parade Song
*(sung to the tune of
"When Johnny Comes Marching Home")*

The *W*s are marching into town. Hooray! Hooray!
The *W*s are marching in a great big *W* parade.
Some have wings and fly around,
Some wear wigs in blond or brown.
Oh, we're so glad the *W*s could come today.

The *W*s are marching into town. Hooray! Hooray!
Some are whistling as they walk our way today.
Some wave wands and grant your wish.
Some wear watches on their wrists.
Oh, we're so glad the *W*s could come today.

Walrus Pattern
Use with "Walrus Puppets" on page 136.

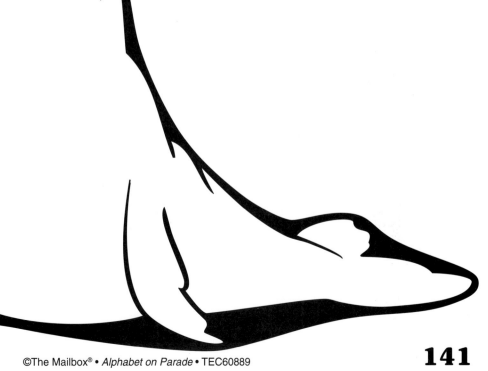

The Letter X

"X-cellent" Xs

This "x-cellent" art project provides extra practice with letter formation. To prepare, cut colorful construction paper into ½" x 2" strips. Give each child an enlarged copy of the *X* pattern on page 147. Have him say the letter as he traces his finger over the pattern. Next, have him cut out the pattern. Then direct him to use the paper strips to form *X*s on the cutout and then glue them in place.

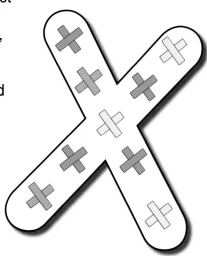

X Is for X Rays

This idea has your little ones taking a look inside the human body and learning about the letter *X* at the same time. In advance, obtain old X rays. Share the X rays with students. Then have each child use a white crayon to draw a skeleton on a white sheet of construction paper. When he finishes, have him paint thinned black tempera paint over his drawing and then set it aside to dry. Wow, what an X ray!

Black

Writing Xs

Give youngsters practice writing *X*s with this quick rhyme. Say the rhyme below as you write an *X* on a chart. Encourage youngsters to join you in several repetitions of the rhyme as they practice writing the letter in the air. Then have each child practice writing *X*s on the sidewalk with chalk, on provided paper, or on dry-erase boards.

> Making *X* is easy.
> I'll show you, if I may.
> First, you make a downward slash
> Then one the other way.

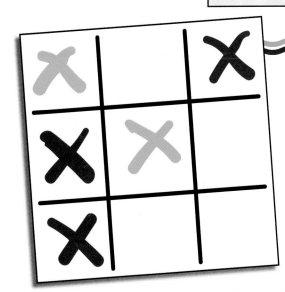

Tic-Tac-Toe

Use a simple game of tic-tac-toe to help your students with letter formation! Instead of having players use *X* and *O* on the game grid, ask them to write only *X*s but to use two different colors.

X Poem

This nifty rhyme is just what you need to help students make the letter-sound connection with *X*. Read the rhyme to your little ones. Then talk about words that begin with *X*, such as *X ray* and *xylophone*. Then introduce youngsters to words that have *X* in the middle or at the end, such as *excellent, extra, box, fox, fix, mix,* and *six*.

> The letter *X* doesn't always sound the same.
> While some letters have one sound,
> There are others *X* can claim.
> In *fix,* the *X* says /ks/.
> It says /z/ in *xylophone.*
> In *X ray,* it just says its name—a sound that's all its own!
> With all these different sounds,
> Learning *X* is extra fun!
> We're so glad that there are three.
> Instead of only one!

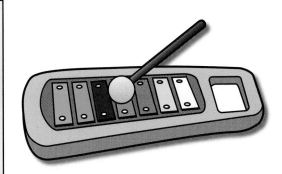

X O X O

Encourage youngsters to send kisses and hugs with this heartwarming idea. First, discuss how *X*s and *O*s are often used to represent kisses and hugs. Then show students how to form each letter. Give each student a strip of construction paper and provide access to a stamp pad. Direct each child to continually press his finger onto the pad and then onto the paper to create *X*s and *O*s as shown. When the paper is dry, have him sign his name and take it home to an extra special person in his life.

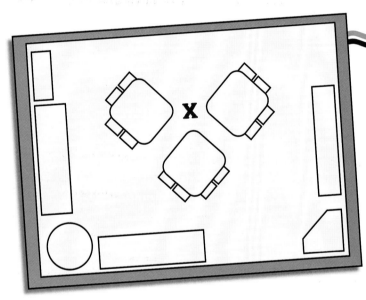

X Marks the Spot

X marks the spot with this letter-recognition activity. Make a large, simple map of your classroom and post it at students' eye level. While students are out of the room, hide a large construction paper *X* pattern in the classroom and mark the spot on the map with a paper *X*. Challenge youngsters to use the map to find the hidden *X*. (For an added challenge, hide other letter cutouts in the room as distractors.) To reuse the activity, simply change the map and rehide the letter cutout.

Water Xylophone

Youngsters will perk up their ears with this investigation. In advance, gather a toy xylophone (or a picture of a real one), six identical drinking glasses, and a pitcher of water. Show students the xylophone and discuss the beginning sound in the word. Fill each glass with a different amount of water and arrange the glasses from the lowest water amount to the highest. Use a metal spoon to gently strike the rim of each glass. Ask students to listen to the different sounds the glasses make. Lead students to determine which glasses make the lowest and highest sounds.

"X-tra" Special Moves

- Make an *X* with your fingers and then your arms.
- Arrange four people on the floor in the shape of an *X*.
- Move to the beat of music played on a xylophone.

X Snacks

- hot cross buns
- sugar cookie dough rolled and arranged to form *X*s and then cooked
- cereal pieces positioned to form an *X*

X Café

Stock your dramatic-play area with items to create an *X* café. Set out materials for students to create signs, placemats, and menus.

The *X* Café Song
(sung to the tune of "Jingle Bells")

X café, *X* café—
Full of special treats.
Let's go out and have some lunch.
It's just down the street.

X buns, *X* toast—
That is what I'll eat.
I just love the *X* café
With all its great *X* treats.

X Parade

Plan an *X* parade with your youngsters! Pick and choose from the following costume and prop ideas. Then teach the provided song and let the marching begin!

Costumes

- skeleton costumes

- X-ray technician lab coats

- masking tape *X*s on clothing

Props

- xylophones

- X rays

- boxes with *X*s marked on them

The *X* Parade Song
(sung to the tune of
"When Johnny Goes Marching Home")

The *X*s are marching into town. Hooray! Hooray!
The *X*s are marching in a great big *X* parade.
Some wear costumes made of bones.
Some are playing xylophones.
Oh, we're so glad the *X*s could come today.

The *X*s are marching into town. Hooray! Hooray!
Some give out *X* kisses as they come our way.
Some have X rays of people and pets.
Some have treasure maps marked with *X*.
Oh, we're so glad the *X*s could come today.

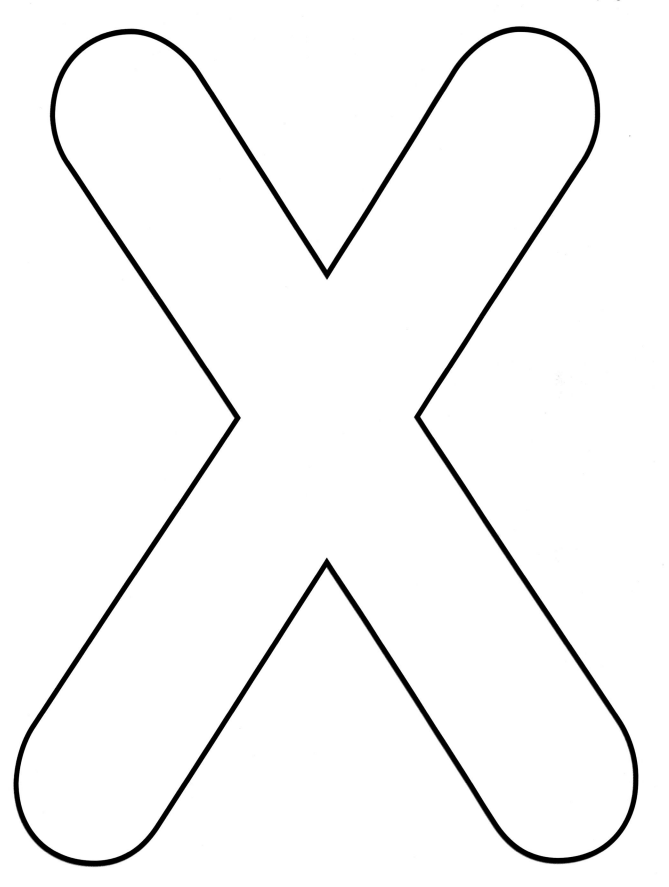

The Letter Y

Yellow Ys

Add sparkle to your letter *Y* activities with this art project. Give each child a white construction paper cutout of the *Y* pattern on page 153. Display a cutout for students and ask them to say the letter and its sound. Then ask them to say the beginning sound they hear in *yellow*. Write the word on the board and circle the beginning letter. Next, have each child paint a *Y* cutout yellow and then sprinkle yellow glitter atop it. When the paint is dry, have her shake off the excess glitter.

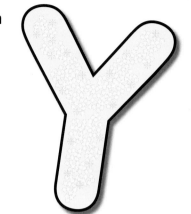

Yak Puppet

Yak, yak, yak—what's a yak? Your little ones will learn that the word *yak* can mean more than just persistent talking when they make this puppet. Make a white construction paper copy of the yak pattern on page 153 for each child. Explain to youngsters the different meanings of *yak*. If possible, show youngsters a picture of a yak. Ask them to say the sound they hear at the beginning of *yak*. Confirm that the word begins with a *Y.* Then give each child a yak pattern to color and cut out. Help each child tape a craft stick onto the back of his yak to make a puppet. Then invite students to use their puppets to yak, yak, yak!

Yarn Art

Students get a feel for the letter *Y* with this letter-formation activity! On the board, demonstrate how to write the letter *Y.* Then give each child a length of yellow yarn and discuss the letter and sound connection in these two *Y* words. Help him cut the yarn into small pieces. Then help him spread glue onto his paper in the shape of a *Y.* Have him place the yarn pieces onto the glue to form the letter *Y.* When the glue is dry, encourage each child to use his fingers to trace his yarn *Y.*

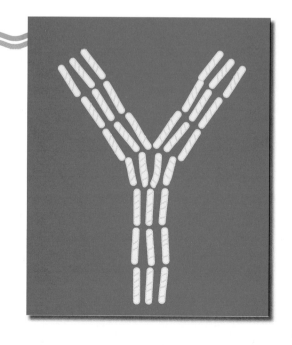

Class Yearbook

Youngsters will certainly feel grown-up when they help create a class yearbook. In advance, gather pictures taken of classroom activities and field trips throughout the school year. Explain to students that a yearbook is a collection of student pictures taken during the school year. If possible, show youngsters a school yearbook. Guide youngsters to say the /y/ sound they hear in *year.* Next, have students help attach the pictures to sheets of white construction paper and then write or dictate a caption below each one. Be sure to include at least one picture of each child. Bind the completed pages behind a student-made cover. Place the resulting yearbook in your reading center or invite students to take turns checking out the yearbook to share with their families.

Yesterday, I rode my bike.

Yakking About Yesterday

What happened yesterday? Ask youngsters to put on their thinking caps to remember past details during this oral language activity. Discuss with students the meaning of the word *yesterday* and emphasize the beginning /y/ sound. Invite one child at a time to tell about one event by completing the sentence "Yesterday, I…" Next, help each child write or dictate her sentence on a sheet of paper. Then ask her to illustrate her sentence. If desired, display each child's sheet on a bulletin board titled "Yakking About Yesterday."

Yes!

Say yes to new friendships with this idea. Share the story *Yo! Yes?* by Chris Raschka with students. Then ask them to name words from the story that begin with the /y/ sound; record their responses. Next, pair each child with someone in the class with whom they do not regularly play. Then, to encourage a new friendship, have the partners talk about their favorite things. After several minutes, help each child write a sentence about his friend, such as "Yes, my friend is Ashley!" Then ask each child to draw a picture of his friend doing her favorite activity to share with the class.

Yes, my friend is Ashley!

Yummy Foods

When it comes to food, children always have an opinion! Use this yummy graph to help youngsters express their feelings about food. In advance, create a chart graph with four different foods as shown. Talk to your group about foods they like and encourage them to say the beginning /y/ sound they hear in *yummy.* Present the graph to students and point out the food choices. Describe each food from the graph and ask each child to rub her tummy if she thinks it's a yummy food. Next, ask her to place a sticky note in the corresponding column on the graph to indicate her choice. Then lead students in counting the sticky notes for each food and comparing the results.

Food	Yummy?
Pickles	☐ ☐ ☐ ☐ ☐ ☐ ☐ ☐
Yogurt	☐ ☐ ☐ ☐
Green Beans	☐
Rice	☐ ☐ ☐

By the Yard

Introduce beginning measurement skills with this small-group activity. Show youngsters a yardstick and explain that it is used to measure length. Encourage each child to say the beginning /y/ sound he hears in *yardstick.* Then give each small group of students a yardstick and challenge the group to find things in the classroom that are about the same length as its yardstick. Later, gather your groups and discuss their results.

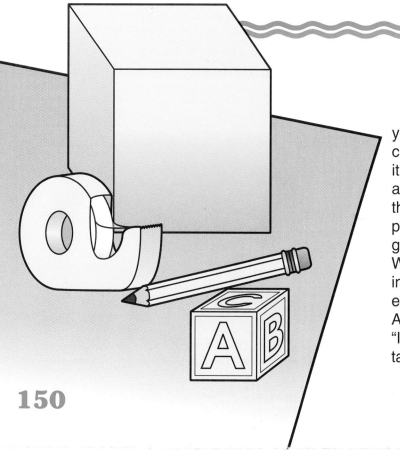

Yellow Detectives

Enlist the help of your little ones to locate yellow items in your classroom. To prepare, cover a large box with yellow paper and place it in the center of the classroom. At circle time, ask students to name a color that begins with the /y/ sound *(yellow).* Invite each child to pretend to be a detective with a magnifying glass and search the room for a yellow object. When he finds one, have him place the object in the yellow box and then sit down. Later, ask each child to retrieve his object from the box. Ask him to make a statement about it, such as "I'm Detective Alex and I found a roll of yellow tape," as he shows it to the class.

150

Y Moves

- Yawn.
- Pretend to yo-yo.
- Do simple yoga stretches. (Use a book or video as a guide.)
- Make a *Y* shape with your body.

Y Snacks

- yogurt (regular or frozen)
- yams
- yellow cake
- yellow banana pudding

Y Café

Stock your dramatic-play area with items to create a *Y* café. Include empty food packages and play foods from the list above. Also, set out materials for students to use to create signs, placemats, and menus.

The *Y* Café Song
(sung to the tune of "Are You Sleeping")

Y café, *Y* café,
Special treats, good to eat.
Yams and yellow pudding,
Yellow cake and yogurt.
Special treats, yummy to eat.

151

Y Parade

Plan a *Y* parade with your youngsters! Pick and choose from the following costume and prop ideas. Then teach the provided song and let the marching begin!

Costumes

- yellow hats

- yellow clothes

- yak headbands
  (Glue a copy of the yak pattern on page 153 onto a headband.)

Props

- yo-yos

- balls of yarn

- yardsticks

- yellow pom-poms
  (Stack ten 1" x 16" strips of yellow tissue paper. Fold the stack in half and roll tape around the fold.)

The *Y* Parade Song
*(sung to the tune
"When Johnny Comes Marching Home")*

The *Y*s are marching into town. Hooray! Hooray!
The *Y*s are marching in a great big *Y* parade.
Some are young, and some are old.
Some wear yellow, oh, so bold!
Oh, we're so glad the *Y*s could come today.

The *Y*s are marching into town. Hooray! Hooray!
Some do yo-yo tricks as they come our way.
Some ride yaks, and some ride yachts.
Some are yelling quite a lot.
Oh, we're so glad the *Y*s could come today.

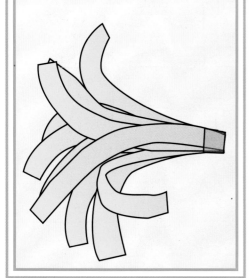

Y Pattern
Use with "Yellow *Y*s" on page 148.

Yak Pattern
Use with "Yak Puppet" on page 148.

The Letter Z

Zany Zebra

Learning about the letter *Z* is in black and white with this painting activity. Make a white construction paper copy of the *Z* pattern on page 159 for each child. Discuss the letter *Z* and encourage students to say the beginning sound they hear in *zebra.* Then invite each child in a small group to paint black stripes on her *Z* pattern to resemble a zebra. When the paint is dry, ask each child to use markers to draw a zebra face on the *Z* as shown. Then have her cut out her zany zebra.

Zebra Puppet

These zippy zebra puppets will add interest to your letter *Z* activities! Give each child a construction paper copy of the zebra pattern on page 159. Write the word *zebra* on a chart and point out its initial consonant. Have students say the /z/ sound. With students' help, make a list of words that have the same beginning sound as *zebra.* Next, have each child color and cut out his pattern. Then help each child tape a craft stick onto the back of his zebra to make a puppet.

Zippy Painting

Zip through letter-formation skills with this fun activity. Gather several different colors of dot art painters or bingo markers. Then cover a table with newspaper and place several shallow containers of water on the table. Invite a small group to the table and give each child a large sheet of white paper. Direct each child to dip a dot painter into water and then press it onto the white paper, causing the paint to splatter slightly. Have him continue in this manner to form a letter *Z* as shown.

Clue Zone

What rhymes with *zoo?* Write the word *zoo* on a chart and help youngsters read the word. Discuss the beginning /z/ sound and the ending sound. Then ask students to think of words that rhyme with *zoo,* and record them on the chart. (Be sure to include the words *moo, new, two, shoe,* and *blue.*) Read one clue from the list below to the class and challenge them to use one of the words from the chart to answer it. Then repeat the activity with each remaining clue.

A cow says _____. *(moo)*
The opposite of old is _____. *(new)*
The number after one is_____. *(two)*
What you wear on your foot is a _____. *(shoe)*
A color word that begins with *B* is _____. *(blue)*

ZOO
moo
new
two
blue
shoe
glue

Zoo Book

Encourage creative thought with this zoo-filled writing idea. Stock your book center with zoo-related stories, such as *If I Ran the Zoo* by Dr. Suess or *Zoo-Looking* by Mem Fox. Read one selection to your class and discuss the /z/ sound youngsters hear in the word *zoo.* Write the sentence starter "If I go to the zoo…" on a chart. Help each child write the sentence starter at the top of a sheet of paper (or have him dictate it for you to write). Have him write (or dictate) to finish the sentence and then illustrate it. Combine all the pages with a student-made cover and staple it together to make a class book. Share the book with the class and then place it in the book center for all to enjoy.

Zip Code Song

Help youngsters learn their zip codes as they sing this zippy song! Repeat the song several times, inserting a different child's zip code in the last line each time.

(sung to the tune of "The Muffin Man")
Do you know your zip code,
Your zip code, your zip code?
Do you know your zip code?
It's [27284]!

155

Zookeeper's Job

Your little zookeepers will zoom to work for the opportunity to take care of the animals in this sorting activity. In advance, gather several sets of plastic zoo animals and mix them up in a tub. Also draw a simple map of a zoo, including areas where each type of animal would live. For example, draw a pen for elephants and trees for the monkeys. During circle time, have youngsters say the beginning /z/ sound heard in *zookeeper,* and discuss the job. Empty the animals from the container and help students sort the animals by type. Then place the zoo map on the floor and ask students to decide where each set of animals would live. Later, place the materials at a center for each child to have an opportunity to be the zookeeper.

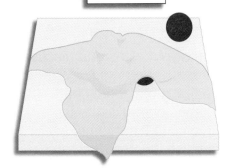

Zip, Zap, Zero!

Introduce youngsters to the concept of zero and practice language skills at the same time with this small-group activity. Write a zero on a chart and discuss the beginning /z/ sound with students. Then place a set of five manipulatives on a table in front of a small group of students. Have the group count the objects out loud and then cover them with a piece of cloth. Secretly remove one object and then remove the cloth. Have youngsters count again and lead them in saying, "Zip, zap, zoom! There are four left." Repeat the activity until there are zero objects left under the cloth. Lead youngsters in saying, "Zip, zap, zoom! There are zero left!"

Zipper Bag Science

Zip up letter-identification skills with these exploratory center ideas. Gather two gallon-size resealable plastic bags. Partially fill one of the bags with water, seal it, and then tape it securely. Then partially fill the other bag with magnetic letters and seal it. Place both bags at a center with an alphabet chart and several magnetic wands. Invite pairs of students to the center. Have one child lay the water-filled bag on top of the alphabet chart on a flat surface. Guide him to look through the water to the magnified alphabet chart. Ask him to find the letter *Z* and then name as many letters as possible. Have the other child place the wand over the letter-filled bag and try to attract the letter *Z* and then name each letter he attracts. Then have the pair switch places and repeat the activities.

Zigzag Z Moves

- Gallop like a zebra.
- Zoom like a roadrunner.
- Zigzag back and forth across a yard.
- Pretend to pick giant zucchini.
- Act zany.

Z Snacks

- zoo animal cookies
- zero-shaped cereal
- zucchini bread
- zucchini slices and dip

Z Café

Stock your dramatic-play area with items to create a *Z* café. Include empty food packages and play foods from the list above. Also set out materials for students to use to create signs, placemats, and menus.

The *Z* Café Song
(sung to the tune of "Yankee Doodle")

Let's go to the Z café
And see what they have for lunch.
Let's go to the Z café
And see what they have to munch.

Zoo crackers and zesty pies,
Zucchini bread, my, oh my!
Let's go to the Z café
And see what they have for lunch.

Z Parade

Plan a *Z* parade with youngsters! Pick and choose from the following costume and prop ideas. Then teach the provided song and let the marching begin!

Costumes

- zookeeper hats

- zippered clothes

- zebra headband
  (Glue a copy of the zebra pattern on page 159 onto a headband.)

- zoo animal mask
  (Cut out eye holes from a paper plate and then decorate it to resemble a zoo animal.)

Props

- stuffed zebra

- toy zoo animals

- zinnia

- tagboard zero

The *Z* Parade Song
(sung to the tune "When Johnny Comes Marching Home")

The *Z*s are marching into town. Hooray! Hooray!
The *Z*s are marching in a great big *Z* parade.
Some have zippers here and there.
Some have zinnias in their hair.
Oh, we're so glad the *Z*s could come today.

The *Z*s are marching into town. Hooray! Hooray!
Some play zithers as they come our way.
Some have zeros in their hands.
Some have zoo animals on headbands.
Oh, we're so glad the *Z*s could come today.

Zebra Pattern
Use with "Zebra Puppet" on page 154.

We're learning about the letter _____!

Here are some ways you can help your child learn about this letter:

_____

_____

_____

- -

Dear Parent,

   We are having a parade to celebrate the letter _____!

Please help us by sending _____

_____

to school with your child by _____. Then come and
                                        date

join us for the fun at _____ on _____!
                              time   date

Thank you for your support!

_____
Teacher